CULTURES OF THE WORLD

Hong Kong

Cavendish
Square

New York

Published in 2018 by Cavendish Square Publishing, LLC
243 5th Avenue, Suite 136, New York, NY 10016
Copyright © 2018 by Cavendish Square Publishing, LLC

Third Edition

Library of Congress Cataloging-in-Publication Data

Names: Kagda, Falaq, author. | Koh, Magdalene, author. | Nevins, Debbie, author.
Title: Hong Kong / Falaq Kagda, Magdalene Koh, Debbie Nevins.
Description: Third edition. | New York : Cavendish Square Publishing, 2018. | Series: Cultures of the world (Third edition) | Includes bibliographical references and index. | Audience: Grades 5-8.
Identifiers: LCCN 2017040196 (print) | LCCN 2017041293 (ebook) | ISBN 9781502632395 (library bound : alk. paper) | ISBN 9781502632401 (ebook)
Subjects: LCSH: Hong Kong (China)--Juvenile literature.
Classification: LCC DS796.H74 (ebook) | LCC DS796.H74 K34 2017 (print) | DDC 951.25--dc23
LC record available at https://lccn.loc.gov/2017040196

Writers, Falaq Kagda, Magdalene Koh; Debbie Nevins, third edition
Editorial Director, third edition: David McNamara
Editor, third edition: Debbie Nevins
Art Director, third edition: Amy Greenan
Designer, third edition: Jessica Nevins
Production Manager, third edition: Karol Szymczuk
Picture Researcher, third edition: Jessica Nevins

PICTURE CREDITS

PRECEDING PAGE
The Hong Kong Observation Wheel dazzles at night.

Printed in the United States of America

CONTENTS

HONG KONG TODAY

LESS THAN A COUNTRY, MORE THAN A CITY—HONG KONG IS AN extraordinary municipality on the coast of southeastern China. Culturally, it's mostly Asian, but partly Western—a global metropolis dense with skyscrapers, teeming with activity, and full of busy people. It occupies more than 250 islands as well as part of the continental Chinese mainland. (Sources often refer to Hong Kong as a city, however, and this book will do so as well.)

Hong Kong has come a long way from its humble beginnings as a fishing village. Today the territory is one of the most crowded cities in the world. Office blocks and apartments jostle for space as streets pulsate constantly with life. But step out of the urban jungle and Hong Kong's serene personality emerges in its quiet green spaces and tranquil Buddhist temples.

That serenity is being tested, however, as Hong Kong now finds itself in a peculiar position. It's like an adopted child who, after many years, is being returned to its birth parents. The city is in a transitional period between these two "families"—a status that is due to run out in 2047. That may seem far off, but the clock is ticking. For some Hong Kongers, that ticking sounds like a time bomb; for others, it's more

Pro-democracy lawmaker Leung Kwok-hung, center, holds a banner calling for true universal suffrage before the election of the Hong Kong chief executive in March 2017.

benign, simply the pulse of history being put right again. Still others don't know what to make of it because the next phase is so uncertain.

In 1997, after 156 years of sovereignty over Hong Kong, the British government handed its colony back to China. The stipulation was that Hong Kong be allowed to hold on to its constitution, maintain its currency and free market economy, and be responsible for its own domestic affairs for the next fifty years. During this time, Hong Kong would be—and now is—a Special Administrative Region (SAR) of the People's Republic of China, under a special "one country, two systems" arrangement. What makes this transition period particularly tricky are the deep differences between those two systems— semi-democratic, capitalist Hong Kong and authoritarian, communist China.

More than twenty years into the arrangement, some Hong Kongers are calling "foul!" Optimists had hoped that acquiring the vibrant city would persuade China to become more like freedom-loving Hong Kong, but just the opposite appears to be happening. Hong Kong has gradually seen its freedoms and civil liberties tamped down. The evidence of this was seen in the 2017 election of Beijing's preferred candidate, Carrie Lam, as the city's leader, Hong Kong's chief executive.

Despite recent demonstrations in Hong Kong calling for full voting rights—the people's power to elect their own leaders—Lam was instead elected by a special 1,200-person committee. Those committee members represent only 0.03 percent of Hong Kong's registered voters, and are said to be mostly elites loyal to Beijing. In 2014, the voting issue had sparked the Umbrella Movement, in which more than one million Hong Kong protesters, advocating for more democratic elections, occupied city streets for seventy-nine days. Hong Kong's constitution, called the Basic Law, itself expresses the goal of full voting rights: "The ultimate aim is the selection of the chief executive by universal suffrage." In the end, those exhilaratingly hopeful demonstrations yielded nothing—except for pushback from an increasingly impatient and disgruntled Beijing. Discouraged, some of the original protesters now advocate for full independence for Hong Kong—a status China is hardly likely to endorse.

Demonstrators hold posters showing some of the missing booksellers in January 2016.

In 2015, events turned ominous when five Hong Kong booksellers suddenly disappeared. The missing men had been selling politically sensitive books in the city. Hong Kong's constitution protects freedom of expression. Article 27 of the Basic Law states: "Hong Kong residents shall have freedom of speech, of the press and of publication ... " As many people at home and abroad feared, the men were discovered to be in China, with implausible explanations as to how and why they were there. Although many questions remain about the mysterious case, it seems clear that the men were abducted by high-level Chinese authorities. In January 2016, British Foreign Secretary Philip Hammond said the incident was a "serious breach of the Sino-British Joint Declaration on Hong Kong and undermines the principle of 'one country, two systems'." (The Declaration, signed in 1984 by then British Prime Minister Margaret Thatcher and Chinese Premier Zhao Ziyang, spelled out the terms of the 1997 handover and guarantees the city's rights and freedoms under the "two systems" formula.)

The flags of China (yellow star) and Hong Kong (white flower) hang together during Chinese President Xi Jinping's visit to Hong Kong in June 2017 to celebrate the twentieth anniversary of its return to China.

Hong Kongers were outraged by the booksellers' arrests, but China's covert—and not so covert—meddling continued. In June 2017, a spokesman for the Chinese Foreign Ministry proclaimed the treaty to be essentially meaningless. "Now Hong Kong has returned to the motherland's embrace for twenty years, the Sino-British Joint Declaration, as a historical document, no longer has any practical significance, and it is not at all binding for the central government's management over Hong Kong. The UK has no sovereignty, no power to rule, and no power to supervise Hong Kong after the handover," he said. For its part, the UK said it had a legal responsibility to ensure China abided by its obligations under the treaty, but it's unclear what Britain could do about it.

Meanwhile, as Hong Kongers worry about—or welcome, as some do—their future with China, the great metropolis has plenty of other concerns. Number one is the extreme and growing disparity between rich and poor. The glittery city is home to more billionaires than anywhere else except New York City. Skyrocketing land and housing prices have forced hundreds of thousands of poor people to live in virtual cages like animals, or in boxes ironically called "coffin cubicles"—so named not only because of the rental units' size and shape, but also the implication that life for the destitute in Hong Kong is a living death. The cost of housing in Hong Kong tops the charts, and those costs have risen 400 percent in the past fourteen years. An apartment of just 128 square feet (11.9 sq meters)—the size of a walk-in closet—easily goes for more than $400,000! Perhaps not so ironically, most of the city's wealthiest tycoons owe their fortunes to real-estate development. And Hong Kong's heralded free economy and low taxes means the government doesn't provide anywhere near enough relief for its lowest-earning workers.

Despite these enormous problems, Hong Kong is a dazzling, energetic city that virtually vibrates with the newest and best of culture and technology. East meets West on its menus, in its languages, arts, and sports, and of course, in its shopping malls and glitzy boutiques. Only time—and the will of its people—will tell what the future holds for Hong Kong.

The interior of the popular Times Square mall in Hong Kong.

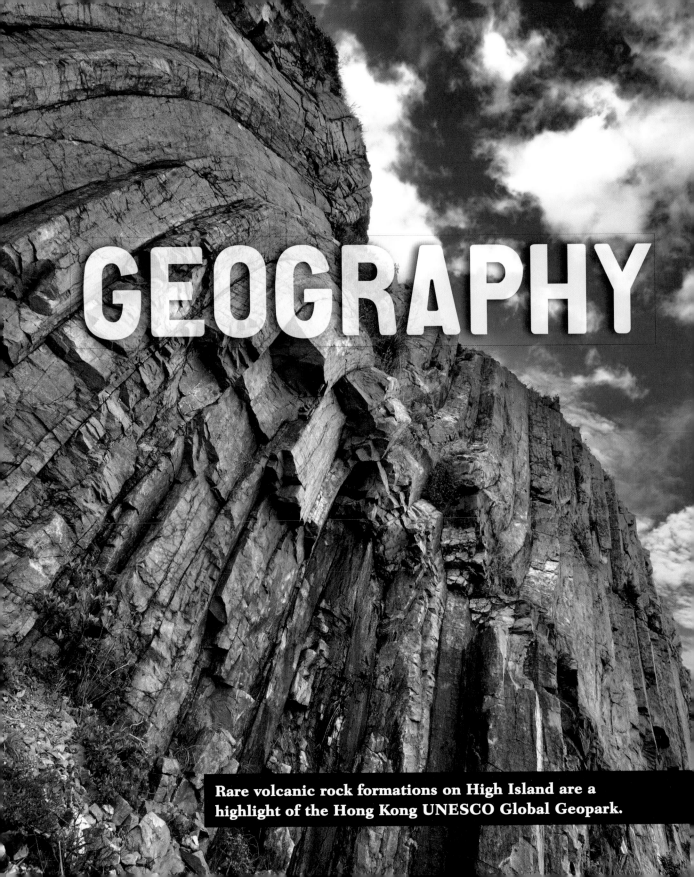

GEOGRAPHY

Rare volcanic rock formations on High Island are a highlight of the Hong Kong UNESCO Global Geopark.

1

HONG KONG IS A UNIQUE PLACE. IT IS a densely-packed urban area, but it's not a city (at least not officially, though it is often referred to as a city). It has mountains, lowlands, cities, and islands, but it's not a country. It's also not a state—in fact, its population is ten times that of Alaska, the largest American state, but its land area is less than half that of the smallest, Rhode Island.

Situated on China's southeastern coast, Hong Kong was a British colony for more than a century, but it's now an autonomous territory belonging to China. It is made up of a section of the mainland and 235 islands of various sizes, with a total land area of 422 square miles (1,092 square kilometer)—about six times the size of Washington, DC.

To the north the Sham Chun River forms Hong Kong's border with the rest of China. The Chinese city of Guangzhou (Canton) is around 60 miles (100 km) away, at the mouth of the Zhu Jiang (Pearl) River. Hong Kong is partially situated in the delta of this river. The territory's other close neighbor is Macao, a Portuguese colony, which is located on the opposite side of the Zhu Jiang River delta.

Although the most common image of Hong Kong is of dense, high-rise buildings, the territory also possesses unusual geological wilderness areas, such as the strange, volcanic rock columns of High Island, off the Sai Kung Peninsula.

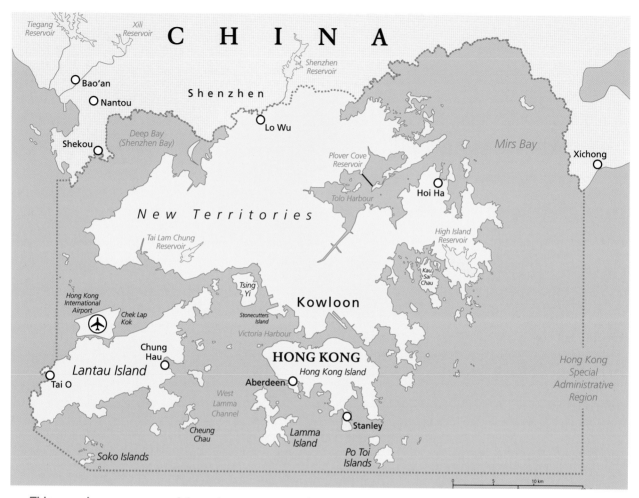

Labels on map:
CHINA

Tiegang Reservoir
Xili Reservoir
Shenzhen Reservoir
Bao'an
Nantou
Shenzhen
Lo Wu
Shekou
Deep Bay (Shenzhen Bay)
Plover Cove Reservoir
Mirs Bay
Xichong
Hoi Ha
Tolo Harbour
New Territories
Tai Lam Chung Reservoir
High Island Reservoir
Kau Sai Chau
Tsing Yi
Hong Kong International Airport
Chek Lap Kok
Stonecutters Island
Kowloon
Victoria Harbour
Chung Hau
Lantau Island
Tai O
HONG KONG
Hong Kong Island
Hong Kong Special Administrative Region
Aberdeen
West Lamma Channel
Cheung Chau
Lamma Island
Stanley
Soko Islands
Po Toi Islands

0   5   10 km

This map shows how Hong Kong spans islands and the Chinese mainland.

Although Hong Kong has no states or provinces, it can be divided into three main regions based on the territory's geography and history. Hong Kong Island was the site of the original settlement. It remains the administrative and economic center. Including its nearby islets, this region covers 35 square miles (90 square km). The Kowloon Peninsula on the mainland and Stonecutters Island, which were the next areas to become part of the territory, cover 10 square miles (26 square km). The New Territories, made up of a large area on the mainland, Lantau Island, and many smaller islands, have a combined area of 377 square miles (976 square km).

Much of Hong Kong is hilly, and a significant amount of the low-lying terrain is made up of land that has been reclaimed from the sea. Only about

12 percent of the land is forested, but small tropical and subtropical plants are abundant elsewhere. Hong Kong's small amount of fertile soil is concentrated in the mainland portion of the New Territories, near Deep Bay.

PHYSICAL FEATURES

MOUNTAINS Hong Kong is part of a partially submerged mountain range. A series of ridges runs from northeast to southwest, with the highest mountain, Tai Mo Shan, rising to 3,140 feet (957 meters). Other mountains include Lantau Peak (3,064 feet/934 m) and Sunset Peak (2,851 feet/869 m) on Lantau Island, Kowloon Peak (1,978 feet/603 m) on the peninsula, and Victoria Peak (1,818 feet/554 m) and Mount Parker (1,739 feet/531 m) on Hong Kong Island. Many of the mountains are composed of volcanic rocks. On the islands the steep slopes drop down abruptly to the sea. Some of the small islands are little more than uninhabited, sea-swept rocks.

Wisdom Path marks the beginning of a climb to Lantau Peak in the hills of Ngong Ing on Lantau Island.

RIVERS The only river of any size in Hong Kong is the Sham Chun River in the north, which forms the border with mainland China. It flows into Deep Bay after collecting a number of small tributaries. Elsewhere in Hong Kong, small streams flow down the sides of the mountain ridges. Reservoirs and catchment systems have reduced the amount of water that is available downstream.

LOWLANDS Flood plains, river valleys, and reclaimed land occupy less than 20 percent of the land in Hong Kong. The largest lowland areas are in the New Territories, north of Tai Mo Shan. This is where most of Hong Kong's farming is done. The main urban areas—the Kowloon Peninsula and coast of Hong Kong Island—take up only around 10 percent of the level land. Land is constantly being reclaimed from the sea. The scarcity of level land has

led Hong Kong's real estate prices, especially in the urban areas, to soar to among the highest in the world.

VICTORIA HARBOR Hong Kong's spectacular deepwater harbor was the major reason that the British chose the site as their trading base in the nineteenth century. The harbor is well protected by the mountains on Hong Kong Island. Hong Kong's administrative center, usually known simply as the Central District, lies on the northwest coast of Hong Kong Island. The city of Kowloon lies on the other side of the harbor.

CLIMATE

Hong Kong lies just south of the Tropic of Cancer and has a subtropical climate. Its seasonal changes are well marked with hot, humid summers and cool, dry winters. Daily temperature averages range from 59°F (15°C) in February to 87°F (31°C) in July.

During the summer Hong Kong is buffeted by the monsoon—a moist, warm equatorial wind built up by pressure systems over the Pacific Ocean. The monsoon brings heavy rainfall between May and August, resulting in floods and mudslides. Typhoons are abundant in summer.

In the winter months pressure builds up over Inner Mongolia, bringing dry, colder winds from the landmass in the west. The dry weather causes water shortages in the cities, forcing Hong Kong to import water from mainland China. Currently the region imports over 80 percent of its potable, or drinkable, water from southern China's Guangdong Province.

An average of 85 inches (2.16 m) of rain falls in Hong Kong each year. More than half of this falls during the summer months between May and September. Only about 10 percent of yearly rain falls from November to March.

FLORA

Many tropical and temperate species of flora are found in Hong Kong. Most of the land area is covered with leafy tropical plants, including mangrove and other swamp plants. The Hong Kong Herbarium, founded in 1878, has about thousands of specimens, including almost two thousand known indigenous species and varieties.

A mangrove forest in Hong Kong.

After centuries of cutting, burning, and exposure, virtually none of Hong Kong's land remained forested. The most common trees are pines, such as the native South China red pine and the slash pine, introduced from Australia. Most of Hong Kong's forest cover, which includes eucalyptus, banyan, casuarina, and palm trees, is the result of reforestation programs started since World War II. Forestry plantations within water catchment areas, country parks, and special areas are managed by the Agriculture and Fisheries Department. Fruit trees, including longans, lychees, and starfruits, are abundant in the New Territories.

Some of the oldest areas of woodlands are the sacred groves found near villages in the New Territories. Villagers have protected these forests because they believe that the trees improve the spiritual and luck-bringing quality of the environment.

A wild monkey sits on a bridge in the Kam Shan Country Park in Kowloon.

FAUNA

TERRESTRIAL MAMMALS Ongoing urbanization has severely disrupted the quiet rhythm of the countryside. Wild mammals are rapidly disappearing from Hong Kong. Occasionally civets, foxes, Chinese leopard cats, and Chinese porcupines may be seen in the New Territories. Leopards and tigers have not been seen for many years. The Barking Deer, a small deer that barks like a dog at night, is now heard only infrequently in wooded areas and is seen even less frequently. Rhesus macaques (a type of monkey), long-tailed macaques, and squirrels can also be found in wooded areas.

BIRDS The Hong Kong Bird Watching Society lists 431 species of birds that have been recorded in the wild. The Yim Tso Ha bird sanctuary, near Starling Inlet, provides a home for herons and egrets. The Mai Po Marshes—an area of mudflats, mangroves, and shrimp ponds in the north—are the richest habitat for birds in Hong Kong.

AQUATIC LIFE Hong Kong has a very diverse marine life. There are an estimated 1,800 different species of fishes in the South China Sea. Clupeoids, croakers, and sea bream are frequently found around Hong Kong. Corals, shelled mollusks, crustaceans, and cephalopods are also common. Marine mammals as well as the Chinese white dolphin, the black finless porpoise, and the bottlenose dolphin are protected under Hong Kong's Wild Animals Protection Ordinance. The green turtle is the only known species of sea turtle that breeds locally.

A Chinese white dolphin.

SNAKES Hong Kong has its share of poisonous snakes, such as kraits, coral snakes, cobras, and vipers. However, most snakes in Hong Kong are harmless.

CITIES, NEW TOWNS, VILLAGES

CENTRAL DISTRICT The City of Victoria—formerly the capital of Hong Kong—is always referred to by Hong Kongers as the "Central District," or simply "Central." It is on the northwest coast of Hong Kong Island and has been the center of administrative and economic activities in the territory since the British settlement in 1841.

Central's dramatic skyscrapers, colonial buildings, and streets lined with shops are constructed on a strip of land along the coast and along the foothills of the mountains behind. Central's stunning view of Victoria Harbor, the city, and the mountains has been immortalized in various paintings and photographs.

KOWLOON On the other side of the harbor is the Kowloon Peninsula, which has undergone great development in recent years. Hong Kong's Kai Tak Airport is located on the eastern fringe of the peninsula. Tsim Sha Tsui, on the tip of the peninsula, is a bustling shopping and nightlife district. Factories, businesses, apartment houses, shops, and markets compete for space. As the peninsula is gradually becoming more crowded, the urban area is spreading northward into the New Kowloon area.

NEW TOWNS As a result of housing pressures on Hong Kong Island and the Kowloon Peninsula, several new towns have been built in the New Territories. These include Tsuen Wan, Tuen Mun, Sha Tin, Tai Po, Fanling, and Yuen Long. Over one-quarter of Hong Kong's population lives in the New Territories, and

over three-quarters of these people live in the new towns. The residents of the densely populated high-rise apartments are catered to by shops, schools, transportation systems, and other services.

The density of Hong Kong's population is evident in this apartment complex on Ma Wan Island in the New Territories.

SMALL TOWNS AND VILLAGES A more traditional style of living continues to exist in villages and small towns. Most of the villages follow the alignment of the river valleys in the New Territories.

INTERNET LINKS

https://www.britannica.com/place/Hong-Kong
This encyclopedia gives a good overview of Hong Kong's geography.

http://www.hong-kong-traveller.com/geography-of-hong-kong.html
This travel site offers numerous helpful maps of Hong Kong's different regions.

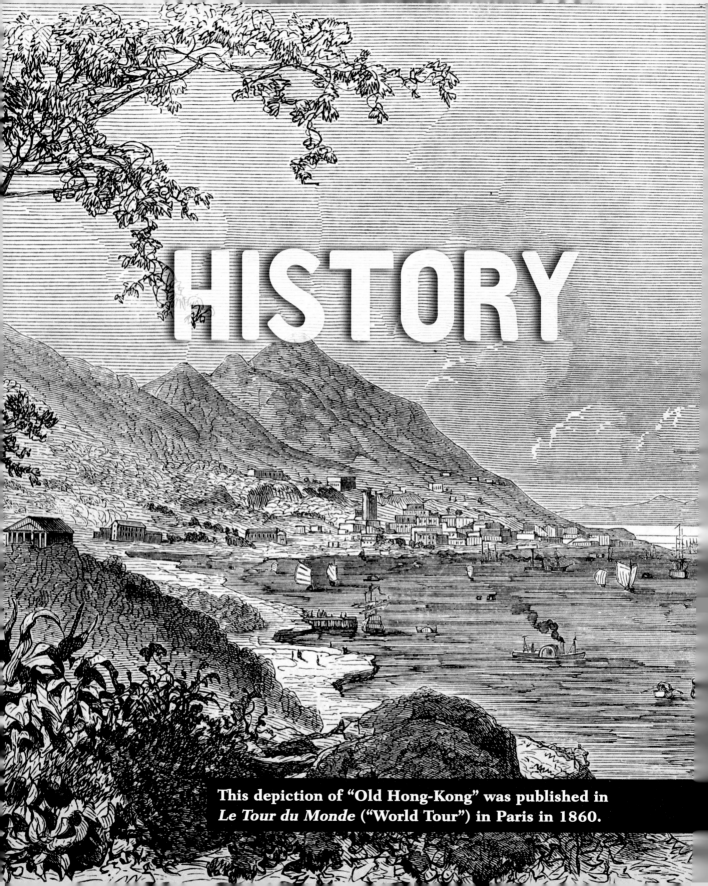

HISTORY

This depiction of "Old Hong-Kong" was published in *Le Tour du Monde* ("World Tour") in Paris in 1860.

2

THERE IS NO QUESTION THAT HONG Kong IS Chinese. And yet, in many ways, it's not fully Chinese. Hong Kong's history has been shaped primarily by two powers— Britain and China. Until the nineteenth century, Hong Kong was not much more than a rocky, sparsely inhabited island off the coast of China. Its modern history began when the British established a settlement on Hong Kong Island in order to initiate trade with China. Hong Kong Island, and subsequently Kowloon Peninsula and the New Territories, became part of a British colony.

During the Ming Dynasty (1368-1644), Hong Kong shipped incense to the Yangzi Valley area. The name of the region, which means "fragrant harbor," may have come from this incense trade.

Hong Kong's growth in the nineteenth and twentieth centuries was dramatic. Lured by economic opportunities, people from mainland China flooded into the colony. Some flocked there to flee from the miseries in their homeland. Despite the outbreaks of war and the Japanese occupation on December 25, 1941, Hong Kong thrived.

But the British colony was never fully British, either. The colony developed its own unique character, shaped by its past—but history, of course, continues on. Hong Kong entered a new era on July 1997, when the British lease on the New Territories expired and Hong Kong reverted to Chinese rule. How the Hong Kong character will adapt to this enormous change remains to be seen, but today, twenty-some years on, the struggle to define Hong Kong continues.

ANCIENT HISTORY

Two Neolithic cultures are believed to have been predominant in the area around Hong Kong from the fourth millennium BCE. Stone tools, pottery, ornaments, and other artifacts have been unearthed in coastal deposits. This suggests that the ancient inhabitants of Hong Kong depended largely on the sea for their survival. There is also evidence of inland settlement. Bronze Age artifacts such as swords, arrowheads, axes, and fishhooks have been found. The discovery of stone molds suggests that the locals worked with metal.

An inside view of the two-thousand-year-old Lei Cheng Uk tomb.

Ancient Chinese literary records refer to a group of maritime people known as the Yue, who occupied China's southeastern coast. The Han Chinese from northern China conquered this region during the Qin (221—206 BCE) and Han (206 BCE—220 CE) dynasties. Many excavations uncovered coins from the Qin and Han periods. Probably the most outstanding find from this period was the brick tomb that was uncovered at Lei Cheng Uk in Kowloon in 1955. Its architecture follows the typical style of Han tomb furniture. Archaeological finds from later historical periods are rare. The dome-shaped limekilns that dot the territory's beaches suggest the importance of lime as a commodity during the Tang Dynasty (618—907 CE).

The first major migration from the north happened during the Song Dynasty (960—1279 CE). However, Hong Kong remained sparsely populated until the nineteenth century. Its coves and islets were ideal hideouts for pirates who plied the South China Sea.

BRITISH TRADE WITH CHINA

In 1553 Portugal established a trading base at Macao, about 40 miles (64 km) away from Hong Kong. Macao quickly became the principal port for international trade with China and Japan. British merchants began trading with China in the late 1700s. In those days, tea imported from Asia had become a favorite drink in England, and the trade was extremely profitable. However, in line with their policy of isolation, the Chinese authorities imposed severe restrictions on the British merchants. They reluctantly allowed a few British merchants to set up offices in the Chinese port of Guangzhou (Canton), but they dictated all transaction terms, accepting only silver and gold in exchange for their tea.

The British soon introduced a new product to tempt the Chinese: opium, a powerful narcotic made from the poppy flower. European sailors brought opium smoking to China in the 1600s. British merchants shipped opium from India to China, where they received gold and silver as payment. By the late 1700s China recorded an estimated two million addicts, and the number was gradually spiraling out of control. Opium addiction drained China's wealth and wreaked havoc across the country. In 1799 China made the opium trade illegal.

In order to get around the trade restrictions imposed by the Chinese, British merchants began to look for a base where they could establish their own trading center. With the outbreak of the Opium Wars in the early 1800s, they got the chance they had been waiting for.

THE OPIUM WARS

In 1839 Lin Zexu, a Chinese imperial commissioner, was sent to Guangzhou to suppress opium smuggling by British merchants. Lin surrounded the British offices with troops, stopped food supplies, and refused to let anyone leave until all opium stocks were surrendered. After a siege that lasted six weeks, Captain Charles Elliot, the British government trade representative, authorized the surrender of 20,283 opium chests.

This nineteenth-century print of the attack on the First Bar Battery in the Opium War between Britain and China has been enhanced with digital color.

This enraged the British merchants, who demanded either a commercial treaty that would put trade relations on a satisfactory footing, or that the Chinese give the British a small island where the British could live under their own flag, without threats from China. Hostilities came to a head when a Chinese man was killed in a drunken brawl between British sailors and Chinese fishermen. Driven out of China, most of the British escaped to the island of Hong Kong. Fighting soon started between the British and Chinese naval forces along the coast. This signaled the beginning of the First Opium War in 1839.

Given its military might, Britain scored an easy victory. China was forced to open a number of Chinese ports to British trade and residence. Besides ceding Hong Kong, the country also had to grant Britain the right to try British citizens who lived in China only within British courts. The decline of the Qing Dynasty ushered in China's defeat in a series of wars at the hands of other European powers, who then received similar privileges based on their military might.

When the British established their settlement in Hong Kong, it was still a rural backwater. The area had twenty villages and hamlets housing a population of about four thousand. Around two thousand fisherfolk lived on boats along the harbor. Hong Kong had only two natural assets—a sheltered deepwater harbor and a strategic location along the trade routes of the Far East.

The Nanjing Treaty, which ended the Opium War of 1839 to 1842, opened up more Chinese ports for British trade, dissolved restrictive trade policies, and allowed the British to station ambassadors in China. The Second Opium War was caused by China's continuing objections to the opium trade and disputes over the interpretation of the earlier treaties. A joint offensive by Britain and France resulted in another defeat for China. The Treaty of Tianjin (then called Tientsin) was signed in 1858, but the Chinese authorities refused to ratify it. Hostilities resumed, and the Western allies captured the capital, Beijing (Peking).

In 1860 China agreed to a treaty with Britain that opened eleven more ports, permitted foreign envoys to reside in Beijing, allowed foreigners to travel in the Chinese interior, and legalized the importation of opium. Kowloon was also ceded to Britain. Other European countries and Japan demanded concessions from China, too. Defeated twice in the Opium Wars, China fell into a century-long period of humiliation by foreign powers.

This drawing illustrates the early British settlement of Hong Kong in the 1840s.

GROWTH OF THE COLONY

After China's defeat in the first Sino-Japanese War (1894—1895), Britain demanded control of the land around Hong Kong for defensive purposes. On June 9, 1898, the New Territories—the area north of the Kowloon Peninsula up to the Sham Chun River, along with 233 outlying islands—was leased to Britain for ninety-nine years. The British faced some opposition when they took over the New Territories, but it soon subsided.

The new settlement in Hong Kong faced severe stumbling blocks at first. Fever and typhoons threatened lives and property. Crime was rampant. The population rose from 32,983 (31,463 Chinese) in 1851 to 878,947 (859,425 Chinese) in 1931. After the Qing Dynasty was overthrown in 1911, many people took refuge in Hong Kong, fleeing the misery in China. The British had not anticipated that the Chinese would choose to live under a foreign flag, so the influx of migrants to the territory took the colonial administration by surprise.

A busy Hong Kong street corner is shown in this 1920 photo.

Despite an unsteady start, the settlement thrived under British rule. Hong Kong became a center of trade with Chinese communities abroad. The late nineteenth and early twentieth centuries saw rapid growth and development in education, health, and social services.

At the end of World War I, strong nationalist sentiments awakened when Germany refused to give its Shantung (Shandong) concessions back to China. The unrest spread to Hong Kong. Because it had the largest stake in China, Britain became the main target of antiforeign sentiment, but that soon changed.

In 1931 Japan occupied Manchuria and tried to take over China's northern provinces. Open warfare broke out in 1937. This marked the beginning of the

Second Sino-Japanese War. Guangzhou fell to the Japanese in 1938, causing a mass flight of refugees to Hong Kong.

WORLD WAR II

Japan entered World War II on December 7, 1941, when its aircraft bombed US warships at Pearl Harbor in Hawaii. At approximately the same time, Japanese aircraft bombed Kowloon, and troops invaded Hong Kong from the Chinese mainland. The Japanese attack forced the British to withdraw from the New Territories and Kowloon to Hong Kong Island. After a week of dogged resistance the defenders on the island were exhausted, and Hong Kong surrendered to Japan on Christmas Day.

The three years and eight months of Japanese occupation were a terrible time for Hong Kong. Trade virtually ceased, currency lost its value, and the

US Navy planes bomb Japanese-held Hong Kong in January 1945.

food supply was disrupted. Government services and public utilities were seriously impaired. Many residents fled to China and Macao. Toward the latter part of the occupation, the Japanese attempted to alleviate the food problems by organizing mass deportations to mainland China.

Soon after the Japanese surrender in August 14, 1945, the colonial secretary set up a provisional government. On August 30, Rear Admiral Sir Cecil Harcourt arrived to establish a temporary military government. Civil government was formally restored on May 1, 1946, when Sir Mark Young resumed his interrupted governorship.

A pro-Communist demonstrator is arrested in Hong Kong in 1967. This is during the time of Mao Tse Tung's Cultural Revolution, which established communism throughout China.

POPULATION GROWTH AND SOCIAL UNREST

With Hong Kong back under British rule once again, those who had fled Hong Kong during the war gradually returned. The population, which had dwindled to about six hundred thousand in 1945, swelled to 1.8 million by the end of 1947.

From 1948 to 1949, as the forces of the Chinese Nationalist government on mainland China faced defeat in the civil war against the Communists, hundreds of thousands of Chinese entered the Hong Kong territory. By 1950 the population reached an estimated 2.2 million.

Hong Kong experienced a period of mounting tension in the 1960s. Social unrest and discontent over poor working conditions began to spread. In 1967 severe riots broke out following a labor dispute at a factory. Inspired by the Cultural Revolution that was sweeping through China, political unrest in Hong Kong soon turned violent. The disruption affected all aspects of life and temporarily paralyzed the economy. However, by the end of the year, the disturbances had been contained. Legislation improved labor conditions and Hong Kong continued to progress peacefully.

THE SARS EPIDEMIC

Shortly after Hong Kong reverted to Chinese rule, it was hit by two devastating crises. One was a severe economic recession. The other was a plague. In 2003 the outbreak of severe acute respiratory syndrome (SARS) brought Hong Kong to a standstill.

The epidemic started in Guangdong, in mainland China, when several live-animal market workers died after being contaminated by the virus from civet cats. (These Asian mammals, which are not cats at all, are considered a delicacy in China.) A doctor who had treated them traveled to Hong Kong, fell ill, and checked into a hospital. He died two weeks later, not knowing that he had infected a dozen guests who had been staying in the same hotel where he had stayed.

Only one of those people infected by the doctor was a Hong Kong resident. Within a week of that man's hospitalization, fifty health-care workers fell ill. Many of the doctors and nurses who were treating these patients also succumbed to the then-unidentified disease, and many of them died.

Meanwhile SARS was racing through other countries, as the infected hotel guests suffered high fevers upon returning home. People who had close contact with them were also stricken with the disease.

The World Health Organization (WHO) issued a global alert as SARS outbreaks were reported in Canada, Singapore, Taiwan, and Vietnam. Patients were often quarantined. The cause—a viral pathogen that was previously unknown in humans—was eventually discovered, and vaccines were developed. By then the disease had already provoked widespread panic and disrupted global travel.

Between November 2002 and July 2003, nearly 8,300 people in 37 countries became ill with SARS, and 774 died. Of those, most cases were in Hong Kong, where 299 people died. No cases of SARS have been reported worldwide since 2004.

SARS wrought damage far beyond its official death toll. The viral pandemic crippled Hong Kong psychologically and economically, as entire communities and lifestyles grinded to a halt.

RETURN TO CHINA

As the British lease on the New Territories neared its expiration date in 1997, concern grew about the territory's future. Formal negotiations between Britain and China commenced in 1982, when British Prime Minister Margaret Thatcher visited Beijing, the capital of China. In 1984 a Sino [Chinese]-British Joint Declaration was signed by the heads of both governments. The agreement stipulated that all of Hong Kong would be returned to China on July 1, 1997. The Chinese government (often referred to as "Beijing") agreed to establish a self-governing Special Administrative Region under its central government. According to the terms of the Joint Declaration, the current social and economic systems would remain unchanged for the next fifty years.

In 1984, British Prime Minister Margaret Thatcher signs the Sino-British joint declaration spelling out the return of Hong Kong to China.

"ONE COUNTRY, TWO SYSTEMS"

China's is a "people's republic"—a communist state. However, it agreed to govern Hong Kong under the principle of "one country, two systems," where the territory would enjoy "a high degree of autonomy, except in foreign and defense affairs" for the specified fifty years. After 2047, presumably Beijing could absorb Hong Kong as another province, subject to the same governance as the rest of the country, but it's too soon to say what will happen then. Beijing's goal seems clear, however, as it continually emphasizes "unity."

Hong Kongers grumble that no one asked them what they would prefer after Britain gave up its dominion. This is true—Hong Kong is not a democracy, especially not now under Chinese rule. However, its citizens do enjoy more civil liberties than do the people in communist China. As the transfer to China drew close, many Hong Kongers feared for their future and emigrated.

Since the handover, Hong Kong's political mood has been largely characterized by conflict between two factions—the pro-Beijing group and the pro-democracy group. Although Kong Kong remains a special autonomous territory, the Chinese government has made it clear that *it* has the ultimate control.

Pro-Beijing demonstrators wave Chinese flags as they disrupt a pro-democracy protest in Hong Kong in June 2017.

INTERNET LINKS

http://www.bbc.com/news/world-asia-pacific-16526765
This very detailed timeline traces the history of Hong Kong from 1842 to the present day.

http://www.cbc.ca/news/world/sars-10th-anniversary-in-hong-kong-brings-vivid-memories-1.1321674
This article looks at the aftermath of the SARS epidemic in Hong Kong.

http://www.lonelyplanet.com/china/hong-kong/history
This travel site offers a quick overview of Hong Kong's history.

http://nationalinterest.org/blog/the-buzz/the-opium-wars-the-bloody-conflicts-destroyed-imperial-china-17212
This article explains the Opium Wars in clear language.

GOVERNMENT

Hong Kong's chief executive, Carrie Lam, answers questions at a meeting of the Legislative Council in Hong Kong in 2017.

3

THE GOVERNMENT OF HONG KONG has experienced a period of great upheaval. Until June 30, 1997, Hong Kong had been a colony of the United Kingdom. A governor nominated in London served as the representative of Queen Elizabeth II. An Executive Council and Legislative Council, which were also nominated rather than elected, decided matters of policy and controlled expenditures.

On July 1, 1997, when the lease of the New Territories expired, Hong Kong reverted to Chinese rule. Under the terms of the Sino-British Joint Declaration, which was signed in 1984, Hong Kong is now a Special Administrative Region (SAR) of China. Although it is part of the Communist People's Republic of China, the SAR's administration retains many features of the British colonial system. Democratic reforms that were introduced by the British in the 1980s and 1990s have also left their mark on the SAR government.

The transition from British to Chinese rule has raised many questions in the minds of Hong Kongers. Issues of self-determination, democracy, nationalism, and cultural identity have been actively debated, and tensions have sometimes erupted into angry protests. Some Hong Kong residents greeted the return to Chinese rule with patriotic enthusiasm, while others were apprehensive about the social and economic changes

● ● ● ● ● ● ● ● ● ● ● ● ●

In 2017, Carrie Lam (b. 1957) became Hong Kong's chief executive. Widely seen as being firmly pro-Beijing, she is the first female leader in Hong Kong's history.

that would result. Some Hong Kongers rushed to obtain British passports to ensure that they would be able to go to Britain if living in the new Hong Kong became too difficult. Others emigrated to the United States, Canada, Australia, and other countries. After the handover, though, many Hong Kongers realized that life under Chinese rule was not as disruptive as they initially feared.

However, there have been some worrisome developments in recent years. Pro-democracy and pro-independence movements have emerged, further polarizing Hong Kong's society. These political factions have annoyed Beijing's authoritarian government so much that, in 2016, it interfered in a local election, which many Hong Kongers found especially alarming. In that case, Chinese authorities refused to allow two outspoken young pro-independence politicians to take their seats on the Legislative Council of Hong Kong after they were elected.

THE COLONIAL GOVERNMENT

The current government of Hong Kong is based on the former colonial system. As a British colony, Hong Kong was administered by the Hong Kong government, which was headed by a governor who was a representative of England's Queen Elizabeth II. An Executive Council offered advice to the governor on important matters of policy. A Legislative Council (known as LegCo) passed laws, controlled public expenditures, and monitored the performance of the government. Two municipal councils (the Urban Council and the Regional Council) provided public health, cultural, and recreational services, and eighteen district boards provided a forum for public consultation.

Until 1985 the governor was appointed by the monarch from England, the Executive Council was appointed by the governor, and the members of LegCo were selected by the governor and the British government. There were no democratic elections. Power was concentrated in the hands of business and political elites, many of whom were expatriates. It was often said that the Hong Kong had a *laissez-faire* government, which means that government intervention in economic matters was minimal. Most Hong Kongers were happy to get on with business and not worry about politics.

THE PEOPLE'S REPUBLIC OF CHINA

Across the border, in mainland China, there is a very different system. The People's Republic of China (PRC) is a communist republic. The Chinese Communist Party (CCP) controls all major governmental institutions. Although China has a legislative body—the National People's Congress—real power lies in the hands of the CCP and the State Council, which are the top executive government organs.

When the CCP came to power in China in 1949, it instituted a communist economic system with central planning, state-run industries, and collectivized agriculture. In an effort to abolish the old social and economic systems, private enterprise and religion were banned. The centralized control of the economy ran counter to Hong Kong's system, which was built on free enterprise and minimal government involvement in trade and industry.

In the 1970s, the Chinese government began to introduce economic reforms and encourage foreign investment and trade. However, China continues to be criticized for its repression of dissidents and its unwillingness to adopt democratic reforms.

For much of Hong Kong's history, the Chinese and British governments tolerated one another and benefited from cross-border trade, even during times of political tension. However, the different styles of government, particularly their approaches to economic affairs, became a major issue in the 1980s and 1990s.

THE TRANSITIONAL PHASE

When Britain and China began negotiating the terms of Hong Kong's reversion to China in the early 1980s, Hong Kongers were made painfully aware of how little say they had in the administration of their territory. Many people felt that Hong Kong was being handed over from one master to another without any input from the people who lived there.

In response to calls for greater participation, the Sino-British Joint Declaration stated that the Legislative Council of the SAR would be elected, but the details of the system were not specified. The first election for the legislature was held in 1985, but only for a minority of seats. Although the Chinese government was unsympathetic toward these belated democratic reforms, the transition seemed to be progressing smoothly.

Meanwhile the Chinese government prepared the Basic Law that would be the mini-constitution of the SAR. Released on April 4, 1990, in the wake of the Tiananmen Square massacre, the Basic Law went into effect on July 1, 1997. The Basic Law made it clear that there would be no territory-wide, freely held elections for all seats. Only one-third of the members of the Legislative Council would be directly elected.

Despite the apprehension that this caused among Hong Kongers, democratic reforms were proceeding in the colony. Political parties were formed, and an election was held in 1991. Prodemocracy candidates won virtually all of the directly elected seats. A new governor, Christopher Patten, was appointed by Britain in 1992. Patten increased the power of the

The political atmosphere in Hong Kong changed suddenly on June 4, 1989, when thousands of people protesting in Tiananmen Square in Beijing, China, were killed, injured, or imprisoned by government soldiers. Known as the Tiananmen Square massacre, the incident caused a furor in Hong Kong. Hundreds of thousands of Hong Kongers filled the streets in protest. Many Hong Kongers supported the dissidents in China, sending money

or helping them escape from China. Hong Kongers feared that freedom of speech and other rights would be lost when China took control of Hong Kong. It was in this turbulent atmosphere that the Basic Law was completed.

Legislative Council and introduced other political reforms despite objections from Beijing. In response the Chinese authorities announced that they would dissolve LegCo in July 1997 and replace it with a provisional Legislative Council.

In March 1993, the Chinese government announced the members of a Preliminary Working Committee, a shadow government that consisted of prominent PRC and Hong Kong political, judicial, and professional figures. As July 1997 drew closer and people began to accept the inevitable reversion to China, support for Patten and his reforms declined.

THE SPECIAL ADMINISTRATIVE REGION

As the leader of Hong Kong's government, the chief executive is appointed by the PRC government in Beijing to serve for a maximum of two five-year terms.

Under the plans outlined during the transition period, the chief executive appoints the Executive Council, the administration secretary, the financial secretary, and the secretary of justice. The Legislative Council has seventy members who serve four-year terms. Thirty-five of these are directly

THE UMBRELLA MOVEMENT

In September 2014, a peaceful student demonstration in Hong Kong's Tamar Park escalated into a massive political protest. It began as hundreds of students gathered to oppose China's proposed reforms to Hong Kong's electoral system—ones that would effectively require candidates to be preapproved by the Chinese government. The students demanded true open elections and more autonomy.

Government officials in both Hong Kong and China condemned the demonstrations as illegal and blamed the West for instigating them. When police tried to clear the demonstrators with tear gas, the heavy-handed tactic backfired, and far more people—not just students—turned out to join the protest. Crowds clogged the streets at major thoroughfares, shutting down Hong Kong traffic. People brought tents and prepared for long-term occupation. People carried umbrellas to protect against both rain and tear gas, and the umbrellas became a symbol of the protests.

Despite numerous arrests, the demonstrations just grew larger. Adding to the chaos, counter-demonstrations also formed, made up of people supporting the police and the government. (There is some evidence that many people were paid to participate.) Meanwhile, Chinese officials banned media from covering the events and censored the internet to clear any references to them.

The confrontation lasted seventy-nine days, and ended without the demonstrators winning any concessions. The event caused a lasting schism in Hong Kong society, as people supported one side or the other. It also resulted in a breakdown of citizens' trust in what had previously been a highly respected police force. In the years since then, some veterans of the Umbrella Movement, as it has been dubbed, have come to feel that the "one country, two systems" concept is not working—they point to Beijing's increasing authoritarian interference and control—and that the only hope for Hong Kong's future is full independence.

In March 2017, one day after Carrie Lam was chosen as Hong Kong's next chief executive, nine leaders of the pro-democracy Umbrella protests were arrested for offenses related to the demonstrations—more than two years after they ended.

elected. The Legislative Council oversees the day-to-day running of Hong Kong, while the State Council in Beijing handles defense and foreign affairs. In the 2016 elections, the pro-democracy parties took 36 percent of the vote, and the pro-Beijing block garnered 40.2 percent (the rest represented smaller constituencies). The next general election is to be held in September 2020.

The Chinese government is unlikely to introduce or support any further democratic reforms.

The new Central Government Complex in Tamar Park, Hong Kong, has been the government's headquarters since 2011.

INTERNET LINKS

http://www.aljazeera.com/programmes/peopleandpower/2017/01/hong-kong-localist-revolutionaries-170118060422170.html
Filmmaker James Leung remembers the Umbrella Movement and what has happened since.

https://www.cia.gov/library/publications/the-world-factbook/geos/hk.html
The CIA World Factbook has up-to-date information on Hong Kong's government.

https://www.gov.hk/en
This is the official web site of the Hong Kong government in English.

ECONOMY

Hong Kong dollars have been the currency of Hong Kong since 1937.

4

UNLIKE CHINA, HONG KONG HAS A free-market economy, at least for now. After 2047, when China's agreement to allow Hong Kong to run its own economy lapses, Hong Kong might be fully integrated into China's communist centralized economy. Or perhaps not. This far in advance, no one is certain what Hong Kong's economic future will be. For now, Hong Kong is following a course of increasing its economic integration with the mainland, particularly in the banking and finance sector. But it maintains its own separate economic system under China's "one country, two systems" principle.

During the 1990s, as Hong Kong's reversion to Chinese rule drew closer, the business community was apprehensive about how Hong Kong's free-market economy would mesh with China's centralized system. Multinational corporations wondered whether they should pull out of Hong Kong and relocate elsewhere in Asia. China put most of these fears to rest with the announcement that Hong Kong's economic system will remain intact for the following fifty years.

Signed in 2003 and updated in 2015, China's Close Economic Partnership Agreement (CEPA) with Hong Kong provides that goods originating in Hong Kong are not taxed. This makes the territory's products more attractive to Chinese consumers than much foreign merchandise. For Hong Kong-based companies, the agreement also improves access to the mainland's service sector.

Hong Kong is a thriving commercial hub, sustained by government policies of free enterprise, free trade, low taxation, and a highly sophisticated transportation infrastructure. For many years, the territory has been considered the world's freest economy.

A LACK OF RESOURCES

Hong Kong is dependent on imports for virtually all of its requirements, such as food, raw materials, consumer goods, capital goods, and fuel. Even water is in short supply. Despite Hong Kong's many reservoirs a substantial proportion of the water consumed by the territory is imported from mainland China.

Hong Kong has no mineral resources to speak of. Graphite and lead mining at Cham Sham (or Needle Hill) and iron ore extraction at Ma On Shan ceased years ago. Small quantities of feldspar are produced for domestic consumption.

Given Hong Kong's sparse forest cover, commercial timber felling is unviable, and there is no potential for producing hydroelectric power from Hong Kong's small streams.

Containers of cargo sit at a busy commercial port in Hong Kong.

AGRICULTURE AND FISHING

As only 5 percent of the land area is arable, agriculture in Hong Kong is limited. Out of this about 40 percent is abandoned or fallow. Less than 3 percent of the population is made up of farmers. Rice cultivation has been replaced by intensive vegetable and pond fish farming, which provide a much greater return on investment. In the New Territories, greenhouses produce fruits, flowers, sweet potatoes, and melons.

Fish ponds dot the landscape outside the city.

Marine fishing is conducted in the waters around Hong Kong. Fishponds occupy 2 percent of the land, and a marine fish culture industry is located in the eastern New Territories.

TRADE AND TOURISM

Hong Kong is one of the world's great trade centers. This is partly because it does not add tariffs to imported goods, and it levies excise duties on only four commodities, whether imported or produced locally—hard alcohol, tobacco, hydrocarbon oil, and methyl alcohol.

Almost half of Hong Kong's trade activity consists of imports—generally raw materials and industrial parts. Clothing, food, machinery, and other consumer goods are also imported, primarily from China and Japan. Other major suppliers include the United States, Taiwan, Singapore, the United Kingdom, South Korea, and Germany.

China is now Hong Kong's main export market. Other major markets include the United States, the United Kingdom, Germany, Japan, and Canada. Re-exports—goods that are imported from one country and immediately exported to another—account for the majority of goods that are shipped from Hong Kong.

Hong Kong is also a major tourist site. Its popularity as an international conference and exhibition site means that almost one-third of its visitors

are business travelers. Tourism is the third-largest source of foreign exchange earnings. After China eased travel restrictions on its own citizens, the number of mainland tourists to the territory surged from 4.5 million in 2001 to 47.3 million in 2014, outnumbering visitors from all other countries combined.

TRANSPORTATION

Because there are limited roads that serve Hong Kong's dense population, the government imposes strict restrictions on car ownership. Compared to other Asian cities, the number of cars in Hong Kong is extremely low. However, there are still enough vehicles to cause traffic jams, which have become a part of commuting life in the Central District and Kowloon.

Double-decker trams wend their way through Hong Kong's streets.

Most commuters use the well-developed public transportation system. An ultra-efficient subway known as the Mass Transit Railway (MTR) connects Hong Kong Island with Kowloon and the New Territories. Passenger and freight rail services to Guangzhou are also available. Other forms of public transportation include buses and electric trolleys. Cable cars operate between Victoria Peak and the Central District, while ferries shuttle people between mainland China and Hong Kong's major islands.

Located on the eastern fringe of Kowloon, Hong Kong's Kai Tak Airport used to be one of the busiest airports in the world. In 1995 more than 27.4 million passengers passed through it. However, Kai Tak could not accommodate increased air traffic. So a new airport was built at Chek Lap Kok, an islet to the north of Lantau Island. Opened in 1998,the new Hong Kong International Airport (HKIA)is the world's busiest cargo gateway and one of the world's busiest passenger airports.In 2015, HKIA handled 68.5 million passengers. The old Kai Tak airport was closed, which provided much relief from noise pollution to the residents who lived within its flight path.

INDUSTRY AND MANUFACTURING

As an international duty-free port, Hong Kong flourished commercially until 1951, when the United Nations (UN) placed an embargo on trade with Communist China and North Korea. Chinese industrialists, many of them from Shanghai, avoided the UN embargo by immigrating to Hong Kong. They brought with them the technology, skilled labor, and capital that catalyzed Hong Kong's rapid industrial development.

Trade between Hong Kong and China later revived. Foreign investment flowed in as manufacturers took advantage of the territory's cheap, abundant labor and the low cost of raw materials from China. In the 1980s, the manufacturing sector employed almost 40 percent of the labor force and became the most important part of Hong Kong's economy. However, its significance has declined. Attracted by lower costs, businesses shifted base to Guangzhou and other Chinese cities. By 2016 industry contributed only

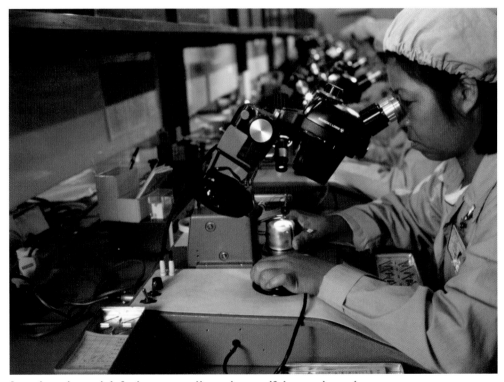

A worker at a watch factory peers through magnifying equipment.

7.2 percent to Hong Kong's economy, and employed only 3.8 percent of its workers.

Emphasis shifted to the production of value-added goods, such as electronics, which require better-skilled labor and command premium prices. The service sector grew to become the gateway to southern China. Hong Kong continues to conduct export operations for facilities that have relocated to the mainland.

People walk past a branch of the Hongkong and Shanghai Banking Corporation (HSBC), a multi-national banking and financial services company.

Hong Kong's strategic position on major shipping and aviation routes led the territory to develop transportation-related heavy industries. Today Hong Kong enjoys an international reputation in shipbuilding and aircraft engineering.

FINANCIAL SERVICES

Hong Kong has developed into the leading financial center in Asia. It ranks third in the world, after New York and London. There is no central bank: The major commercial banks and the government-run Banking Commissioner's Office work together to manage the territory's currency and interest rates.

Hong Kong's pro-business environment is reflected in its sophisticated financial infrastructure. A wide range of services is easily available, and there are no restrictions on foreign exchange. Such features have attracted many foreign banks, and 85 of the world's 100 largest banks are represented in the territory.

Domestic and international currencies are traded at the Hong Kong foreign exchange market. The fifth largest in the world, it has a daily turnover of over $90 billion.

Although Hong Kong's commercial openness is a draw, Hong Kong is vulnerable to regional fluctuations and global changes. Because of its heavy dependence on foreign trade and financial services, the global economic recession of 2008—2009 caused its economy to contract; however, it has recovered since then. In fact, the territory's economic performance in 2017 was even better than predicted with 4.3 percent growth in the first part of the year.

Property prices continue to skyrocket, however. Credit expansion and a tight housing supply have caused Hong Kong property prices to rise rapidly; consumer prices increased 4.4 percent in 2014, but slowed to 2.9 percent in 2015. Lower- and middle-income segments of the population are increasingly unable to afford adequate housing.

INTERNET LINKS

http://www.hkeconomy.gov.hk/en/home/index.htm
The Hong Kong government provides up-to-date economic information on this site.

http://www.hongkongairport.com/eng
This site provides facts and figures about Hong Kong International Airport.

ENVIRONMENT

Hong Kong's polluted air is evident in this view from the

5

W ITH HONG KONG BEING ONE OF the world's most densely populated places, it's no surprise that its environment faces great challenges. Rapid industrialization and development impacted the territory's air, water, and soil, as well as plant and animal life. Millions of human beings crammed into a small space create enormous volumes of all sorts of waste—liquid and solid sewage, municipal trash, and industrial byproducts, some of which are toxic. Even noise pollution is common grievance. Of all these serious environmental concerns, air pollution is Hong Kong's most critical problem.

Air does not stop at political borders. Much of Hong Kong's air pollution drifts across the border from China. About 60-70 percent of the particulate matter in the air comes from the mainland. In winter, when the winds blow more forcefully in Hong Kong's direction, as much as 77 percent of the dust in the city's air comes from China.

AIR POLLUTION

Like any large urban city, Hong Kong faces immense threats from air pollution. Vehicle emissions, especially from diesel-fueled engines, are a pressing problem. Factories in the Pearl River delta spew pollutants that often blanket the region in smog. Since the late 1990s, Hong Kong's Air Pollution Index has regularly exceeded the dangerous level of 100.

The threat to public health is dire. Asthma and chronic bronchitis are rampant. A landmark study in 2016 found that air pollution increased the risk of dying from any type of cancer by 22 percent in Hong Kong. Not surprisingly, the hardest hit neighborhoods—for bad air and its resulting health problems—are also the poorest ones, where housing and traffic are the densest.

The extreme density of Hong Kong's high-rise buildings prevents sufficient air flow, traps traffic-related pollutants at street level, and causes the temperature to rise. Tens of thousands of old diesel vehicles still remain on the roads despite government programs to encourage more efficient models. Container ships docking at Hong Kong's busy port are allowed to burn high sulfur fuel, and the territory's power plants run almost entirely on fossil fuels—52 percent of the plants use coal to provide the city's energy.

Environmental activists complain that the government moves slowly, if at all, to address the issue. Since the city's wealth has come largely from its hands-off business atmosphere, officials are reluctant to enforce regulations that will threaten trade. A former chief executive, Donald Tsang (in office 2005—2012) famously downplayed the city's air pollution problem when he asserted that Hong Kong had the world's highest life expectancy at birth (in 2016 it ranked number 7), which proved it was "the most environmentally friendly place for people, for executives, for Hong Kong people to live."

Nevertheless, the government has made some efforts to encourage the use of cleaner fuels and vehicles. In 2005 nearly all of the territory's 18,000 taxis and light buses switched to liquefied petroleum gas (LPG)—a cleaner alternative to conventional diesel fuel. Hong Kong is also the first Asian economy to sell ultra-low-sulfur diesel, a motor fuel that releases fewer sulfur dioxide pollutants. Financial incentives are given to people who use environmentally friendly modes of transportation.

Besides diesel vehicles, electricity-generating power plants add pollutants to the air. The Environment Protection Department (EPD) caps the emission levels of furnace installations and large industrial facilities. However, those allowable levels are three and half times higher than those recommended by the World Health Organization (WHO). Nonetheless, the EPD reported that concentrations of major air pollutants had fallen about 30 percent between 2012 and 2016.

There are no easy solutions for the regional smog problem. Many Hong Kong businesses have factory operations in nearby Guangzhou, China, which blatantly flout environmental regulations. To combat air pollution on a larger scale, Hong Kong will need the assistance of the mainland.

NOISE POLLUTION

City dwellers worldwide suffer from noise problems, including road traffic noise. Hong Kongers probably face worse noise than many of their global counterparts. Hong Kong's narrow streets, densely built-up spaces, and constant human activities generate a constant cacophony every day.

Direct measures to reduce the excessive din include adjusting road alignment, resurfacing roads with low-noise materials, and erecting noise barriers. Legislation was tightened in 2002 to ensure that new vehicles complied with internationally recognized noise standards. Permits for construction regulate the use of heavy equipment at night and during public holidays to alleviate the problem.

SOIL EROSION

Hong Kong's rugged terrain and high population pressures mean there is little land available for cultivation. The original forest vegetation had already been cut or burned by the 1800s. Wooded hills cover only one-fifth of Hong Kong, while grasslands, badlands, and swamps account for over half of the territory's total area.

The region's heavy rainfall makes matters worse. Sparse vegetation and limited forest canopy expose unprotected land to frequent downpours. Nutrients are leached from the soil, making it poor and unsuitable for

Congested traffic at rush hour in downtown Hong Kong is an everyday occurrence.

agriculture. With no plant roots to bind the earth, large tracts of land are easily weakened and swept away. During summer, soil erosion on slopes occurs regularly. Roads and drainage systems are blocked, leading to floods, property damage, business losses, and severe inconvenience for the local people.

WATER QUALITY AND SEWAGE TREATMENT

Water quality in Hong Kong's assorted rivers and bays is erratic. Small streams and tributaries around water catchment areas are cleaner than larger water bodies, such as Inner Deep Bay and Victoria Harbor. The territory's population growth—expected to reach 8.89 million by 2039—will put greater pressure on water quality.

Around 70—80 percent of Hong Kong's fresh water is piped in from the Dongjiang (Dong River) intake to the Shenzhen Reservoir in neighboring Guangdong province by way of a dedicated aqueduct. The need for freshwater is partly alleviated by the use of seawater for toilet flushing, using a separate distribution system.

Untreated sewage that is dumped into open waterways pollutes the numerous seas and bays that surround Hong Kong. In addition to having a bad stench, bacteria in the water can make swimmers ill, contaminate aquatic life, and kill marine species. Pollution from agricultural runoff and human activities also breeds red tides. These toxic algae infestations have wiped out varieties of fish that used to swim near the main islands. This has forced fishermen to venture farther from shore in search of their catch.

To improve water quality the Environment Protection Department (EPD) controls the wastewater discharge. Factories have to meet specified discharge standards before they are given a license to continue disposal operations. Established in 2001, the Harbor Area Treatment Scheme (HATS) delivers sewage from Victoria Harbor to Stonecutters Island for disinfection and for chemical and biological treatment. Since the facility was built in 2001, it has reduced the amount of E. coli bacteria in the nearby water by 99 percent, while other pollutants have been reduced by 70—80 percent, allowing coral to return to Victoria Harbour. Hong Kong's beaches became safe for swimming again. A similar system in Tolo Harbor has reduced the occurrence of red tides. About 70 percent of the sewage produced daily is treated.

WASTE MANAGEMENT

In 2015, the average Hong Konger disposed of about 3 pounds (1.36 kilograms) of garbage daily. About 5.5 million tons (5 million metric tons) of waste are disposed of each year in three strategic landfills, where about 43 percent of the solid waste is household trash, 28 percent is construction waste, and 24 percent is commercial and industrial waste. There are thirteen closed landfills in Hong Kong, which the government has restored—or is working to restore—to usable land, such as parks and recreational facilities.

A recycling scrap yard on the coast.

Meanwhile, the three remaining landfills are approaching their limit, which should occur by around 2019. In an effort to cut down on the amount of trash the government has introduced various schemes such as recycling plants, but so far the endeavors have been insufficient. The EPD is planning to build an incinerator on Lantau, the largest of the territory's islands, which will be able to burn about 30 percent of the city's waste. However, given Hong Kong's air pollution problem, many citizens oppose the measure. Another solution, to be implemented in 2019, is the imposition of a "waste charge" per volume of trash per household. When citizens are forced to pay for the collection of their garbage based on its volume, they will likely take seriously the need to reduce the amount of waste they generate.

RECYCLING Hong Kong has facilities for recycling, but needs more. The collection, reprocessing, and export of recyclables are undertaken by private enterprises, which are often hampered by inadequate logistics, financing, and infrastructural support.

To encourage households to separate waste that can be recycled, voluntary organizations work with the Food and Environmental Hygiene Department (FEHD) to build recycling bins at public parks, commuting points, and building entrances. However, governmental support for such initiatives is patchy.

Public agencies can endorse the green movement by being more proactive toward resource conservation and producing less waste. Providing economic incentives for people to recycle more and discard less is another option. Advancing the concept of environmental citizenship, both from the top down and at the grassroots level, takes time, but the rewards are long-term.

PROTECTED AREAS

Twenty-four country parks and other specially protected areas cover about 43 percent of Hong Kong's total land. Many scenic hills and woodlands are planted with fire-resistant trees such as acacia and eucalyptus. Development is tightly controlled around these areas. Litter is collected frequently. Educational and recreational facilities, such as hiking trails and camping sites, are clearly marked. In 2011, about 13.5 million people visited the parks.

Although smaller in scale, Hong Kong's four marine parks and its sole marine reserve are no less important. Spread over 6,005 acres (2,430 hectares) the coastal areas and seascapes sustain a host of conservation and research studies. Fishing is completely banned in the marine reserve. Only local villagers are permitted to fish within marine parks.

ECOFRIENDLY LEGISLATION

Hong Kong has several laws to protect nature. The Agriculture, Fisheries and Conservation Department (AFCD) has the job of conserving ecological resources and enforcing legislation.

Entry to wildlife habitats such as the Mai Po Marshes, Sham Wan, and Yim Tso Ha Egretry is heavily restricted. The sale, export, and possession of protected animal species are prohibited. Rare plants such as azaleas and Hong Kong's native bauhinias are guarded under the Forests and Countryside Ordinance. The use of explosives, toxic substances, or other destructive fishing practices is illegal.

HONG KONG WETLAND PARK

To promote environmental appreciation among the public, Hong Kong opened its first major green tourism facility in 2006. The Wetland Park at Tin Shui Wai reconstructs the natural
habitats of waterfowl, native species, and other types of wildlife. Spanning a 148-acre (60 ha) Wetland Reserve and Wetland Interactive World, it expects to draw more than a million nature lovers annually.

The attraction offers intimate peeks into Hong Kong's ecological diversity. Visitors can step into the world of the green turtle, or watch the endangered black-faced spoonbill bird take flight. Many people also drop by to greet the park's reptilian resident, a female crocodile that is affectionately named Pui Pui, which means "precious one" in Cantonese. The crocodile rules over a deluxe home that is equipped with a heated pool, a landscaped enclosure, and weighing scales.

INTERNET LINKS

http://www.bbc.com/future/story/20170427-hong-kong-has-a-monumental-waste-problem
This BBC article provides a serious look at Hong Kong's enormous waste situation.

http://www.epd.gov.hk/epd/english/top.html
This Environmental Protection Department site has a wealth of information about Hong Kong's environment.

http://www.wetlandpark.gov.hk/en/index.asp
The site of the Hong Kong Wetland Park includes information about Pui Pui.

http://www.wsd.gov.hk/en/home/index.html
The Hong Kong government Water Supplies Department site has a wide range of water information.

HONG KONGERS

A young woman smiles with the Hong Kong skyline in the distance.

6

T HE PEOPLE OF HONG KONG ARE referred to as Hong Kongers, or less commonly, as Hong Kongese. Though they are overwhelmingly ethnic Chinese, Hong Kong is a cosmopolitan city and an international business center. As such, it naturally is home—permanent or temporary—to people from all over the world. In fact, Hong Kongers were multiracial from the very start, a reflection of the diverse nature of the British Empire. For example, when Britain took possession of Hong Kong in 1841, there were almost three thousand Indian soldiers among the British troops.

Since then Hong Kong has absorbed people from all over the world. The ethnic Chinese form the majority of the population. There is, of course, also a British community. In its early days Hong Kong also attracted immigrants from the United States, Germany, Portugal, and Denmark, as well as Hindus, Muslims, Parsis, and Sikhs from India, and Jews from Iraq. There are also Hong Kong—born Eurasians, people of mixed European and Asian heritage.

A 2011 poll of Hong Kongers found that less than 20 percent identify as Chinese; 38 percent identify as a Hong Konger; and 43 percent identify as a "Hong Kong Chinese." The identification with "Hong Kong citizen" reached a ten-year high, while that of "Chinese citizen" dropped to a twelve-year low. The least popular suggested cultural identity listed on the survey—even below "global citizen"—is "citizen of the PRC (People's Republic of China)."

Shops stay open until midnight in the Mong Kok area, one of Hong Kong's major shopping areas, attracting crowds on a December night.

The original communities that populated Hong Kong boasted people from all walks of life. They were traders, lawyers, missionaries, shipbuilders, shopkeepers, soldiers, journalists, editors, bankers, and artists. Many of their descendants live in Hong Kong today. They are equally fluent in English and Cantonese. A turbaned Sikh man speaking fluent Cantonese would not merit a second glance in Hong Kong. Smaller communities have managed to keep their distinct identities and traditions alive while adapting to the dominant culture.

Today Hong Kong has a population of about 7.2 million. About 93 percent of the population is ethnic Chinese, with Indonesian, Filipino, and other Asians and non-Asians making up the rest.

The territory has a population density of around 17,400 people per square mile (6,700 per square km). Some sections, such as Kowloon's Mong Kok district, house 40,000 people per square mile (100,000 per square km), making them the most densely populated areas on Earth.

THE HONG KONG CHINESE

The overwhelming majority of Hong Kongers are Chinese. About one-third of Hong Kong Chinese were born in China. The Chinese population can be subdivided into groups based on which part of China they (or their ancestors) came from, and which dialect they speak.

CANTONESE Most of the early Chinese immigrants came from the southern Chinese province of Guangdong. They brought with them their dialect, Cantonese, and their customs. Hundreds of thousands of immigrants from Guangdong entered Hong Kong during the first half of the twentieth century. Today around 90 percent of Hong Kong Chinese are of Cantonese descent.

Over the years the Hong Kong Chinese have created their own identity, which sets them apart from the Chinese of China or Taiwan. Because they have lived under British influence for so many years, they are perceived as being more Westernized. The Hong Kong Chinese were enjoying the material benefits of modernization, such as television and indoor plumbing, long before these things were available in China or Taiwan. However, this modern veneer has not eliminated their cultural attitudes and traditions, which continue to remain very Chinese.

When Hong Kong was a British colony, the Hong Kong Chinese asserted their distinct identity by retaining their Cantonese dialect, rather than adopting Putonghua, the national language of China and Taiwan, which is based on Mandarin, the dialect spoken in Beijing and other parts of China. They also refused to adopt the simplified Chinese characters used in China. However, following the handover to China, the Hong Kong Chinese have started to learn Putonghua and are now using simplified characters in addition to traditional characters.

OTHER DIALECT GROUPS A minority of Hong Kong Chinese—less than 10 percent—come from other dialect groups. These groups include the Hakka, Siyi, Chaochow, Hoklo, and Tanka. There are also significant numbers of Chinese from Shanghai and Fukien in China, and from Taiwan. There are smaller numbers of people from all over China. Almost all of them live a modern, urban lifestyle, but their heritage is revealed in the dialect they speak among themselves and the details of their cooking, ceremonies, religious practices, and other customs. The few people who retain a more traditional lifestyle, such as the Hakka farmers of the New Territories, may also have a distinctive style of dress.

OTHER ETHNIC GROUPS

Around 6 percent of the population of Hong Kong belongs to ethnic groups other than Chinese. There are roughly equal numbers of Asians (including Indians, Filipinos, Japanese, and Pakistanis) and non-Asians (including British, Americans, Australians, Canadians, and New Zealanders). Some are descended from early settlers in Hong Kong, while others live in Hong Kong as expatriates (people who live outside their native country by choice).

In Hong Kong the term *expatriate* was once used to describe all non-Chinese, even those who were born in Hong Kong. Ethnic Chinese were not considered foreigners, even if they were born outside of Hong Kong. This attitude changed slowly as Chinese Hong Kongers saw many non-Chinese residents becoming fluent in Cantonese, contributing to the territory's economy and administration.

However, non-Chinese Hong Kongers were made to feel like foreigners in their own land when it was announced that only ethnic Chinese would be given Chinese citizenship in July 1997, when Hong Kong reverted to China. Some people whose families had been in Hong Kong for generations faced the prospect of becoming stateless. Those who have been fortunate enough to obtain British citizenship are able to remain in the Special Administrative Region. They can leave anytime they want. These people have adopted a wait-and-see attitude. Those who were not so fortunate have had to leave the only home they have ever known, emigrating to the United States, Canada, Singapore, and Malaysia, among other countries.

A Chinese government poster announces changes in immigration policy that will affect British citizens.

INDIANS Indians are a prominent group in Hong Kong's commercial and social scene. In the late nineteenth and early twentieth centuries, Indian traders, mostly Dawoodi Bohras from Bombay and the state of Gujarat, came to Hong Kong in large numbers. At first they worked with British traders, and later they set up business for themselves. They were joined by other Indian traders, such as Muslims, Hindus, and Parsis.

Although the traditional occupation of most Hong Kong Indians is trade, the Sikhs usually came to Hong Kong as part of the British police or military force. Even today Sikhs have the reputation of being incorruptible. Hong Kong's organized crime syndicates know that Sikhs cannot be enticed to rob their employers. For this reason, and because they are generally sturdy in their physical build, Sikhs are often employed as guards.

Although most Hong Kong Indians still continue to work in trade, many third- and fourth-generation Hong Kong Indians have branched out into other occupations, ranging from academia and banking to the civil service.

JEWS Among the earliest settlers in Hong Kong were Sephardic Jews from Iraq. Sephardic Jews follow the Jewish liturgy and customs of medieval Spain

and Portugal. In the fifteenth century, they were expelled from Europe and settled in the Middle East and North Africa.

Iraqi Jews were traders who came to Hong Kong and China by way of India. This merchant community enjoyed close personal and commercial ties with the Jewish communities in Shanghai and Bombay. Initially trading in cotton and other commodities, the Jews soon became involved in the opium trade. Eventually they branched out into other areas, including real estate, banking, insurance, and hotels. This propelled them to power and influence, both within Hong Kong and on the international business scene. Lord Lawrence Kadoorie, a member of Hong Kong's Jewish community, was the first person from Hong Kong to have a seat in the United Kingdom's House of Lords.

EURASIANS Eurasian communities can be found in all the Asian countries that were colonized by Europeans. The word *Eurasian* reflects the mixed heritage of those descended from the union of European and Asian parents. Eurasian communities have distinct traditions, cuisine, and customs that differ slightly, depending on the ethnic groups from which they were descended.

Interracial relationships were frowned upon in the early years, and Eurasian children of mixed-race marriages faced considerable discrimination. The separate ethnic communities in Hong Kong were not comfortable with the idea of mixed marriages. However, since Eurasians were usually fluent in English, Cantonese, and possibly the other languages of their parents,

More than five hundred Jewish Hong Kong residents, wearing traditional Chinese dress, pose for a group picture at their synagogue.

the British colonial administration used them to fill posts in the civil service. Many Eurasian families in Hong Kong are among the island's wealthiest and most respected inhabitants.

In recent years a new Eurasian community has grown. Many Hong Kongers have traveled abroad for work or study and have brought home European or American spouses.

INTERNET LINKS

http://www.census2011.gov.hk/en/main-table/A205.html
The results of the 2011 census are listed on this page.

https://www.nytimes.com/2014/10/08/world/asia/hong-kong-people-looking-in-mirror-see-fading-chinese-identity.html
This *New York Times* article examines how Hong Kongers define their identity.

LIFESTYLE

Crowds fill the streets in a busy shopping district.

7

LIFE IN HONG KONG IS *FAST*. PEOPLE walk fast, talk fast, and eat fast. Time is money, as the saying goes, and it can seem that everyone in the city is in a hurry to make more. Life in Hong Kong is crowded. Streets are jammed, sidewalks are packed, and subway cars are crammed tighter than sardine cans. The concept of personal space has a different meaning when people have to endure such close and constricted spaces. The city absolutely buzzes with noise and activity, but most Hong Kongers have learned to deal with life in one of the most densely populated places on earth.

Hong Kong was carved out of a rocky island by people with ambition, determination, and the desire to succeed economically. This motivation is reflected in Hong Kong's fiercely competitive business world. At the same time traditional Chinese values and customs play an important role in everyday life.

"Face," meaning one's publicly projected dignity or sense of value, is an important concept in Chinese society. "Keeping face" means upholding one's prestige in society. "Losing face" is avoided at all costs. A person could lose face by being ridiculed or reprimanded in public, which would result in a loss of prestige. "Giving face"—treating others with due respect—is something children learn from a young age.

FAMILY

The family is the strongest social unit in Hong Kong. Children are taught that respecting their family and parents is their primary duty. This ensures that the family remains close knit.

In the old days, the traditional family structure consisted of an extended family that lived together under one roof. However, given Hong Kong's space constraints, large families are no longer the norm. It is now common for children to move to their own apartments when they marry and begin to raise a family.

In the traditional family, the man was the head of the household. His word was law. He went out to earn a living while his wife tended to the home and children. Now that more women are educated, working, and financially independent, conventional gender roles are changing. Women are challenging traditional thinking about their homebound status. The role of the household head is also changing. Children no longer accept the father's absolute authority. Today children often expect to have a say in family matters.

Three generations of a Hong Kong family relax in a park.

Grandparents are also affected by such social changes. In the traditional extended family, grandparents were considered the keepers of wisdom; their opinions were sought and respected. Because many members of the elder generation now live apart from their children and grandchildren, grandparents' influence on the family has decreased.

High-rises house people in very tight quarters.

HOUSING

Housing has always been a problem in Hong Kong. Some 40 percent of the territory's land area is unsuitable for development; so as a result, most Hong Kong residents live in high-rise apartments. Only the very wealthy reside on landed property. Many of these residences are mansions scattered in and around the southern hills of Hong Kong Island. Members of the middle class live at the base of the hills in cramped 1,000-square-foot (92 sq. m) apartments that rent for more than $3,000 US dollars a month; which cost about $1.5 million and up to buy.

As Hong Kong developed and its population grew, housing costs rocketed out of the average resident's reach. Hundreds of thousands of people lived in squalid shantytowns. In 1953 a shantytown fire left fifty-three thousand people homeless. The government's emergency relocation measures soon became a full-scale public housing program. Construction on a massive scale produced multi-story apartment blocks that dot the landscape today. The overcrowded apartment blocks are generally an improvement over the old shantytowns—but in some ways, they might actually be worse in that they cram even more bodies into small spaces.

The government's Hong Kong Housing Authority (HKHA) and the Hong Kong Housing Society (HKHS), a non-governmental organization, work to provide people with homes. The HKHA also finances the construction of

Unquestionably Hong Kong's worst form of housing, and its deepest shame, is the so-called "cage home." Exact figures are unknown, but between fifty thousand to two hundred thousand people are thought to be living like animals in tiny cages or boxes. The Hong Kong government rather euphemistically refers to these rental units as "bedspace apartments."

In this densely packed city, rents are so exorbitant that the lowest-paid workers often can't afford even the smallest, most dismal of apartments, or even a room. In the poorest parts of town, old apartment buildings have been subdivided, often illegally, into as many tiny units as the landlord can fit. In the worst cases (and there are many), these units are cages measuring just 6 feet long by 2.5 ft wide (1.8 m x 0.76 m)—barely room for an adult man to lie down, and often not high enough to sit up in. The cages are stacked two and three high, with twenty or even thirty crammed into one suffocatingly small room.

Those units that have solid walls rather than cage wire are sometimes called "coffin cubicles." The inhabitants of these cages and boxes are usually single men, but they also include the elderly, the mentally ill, single mothers, and children. Residents have to share bathroom and kitchen facilities (if any)—typically an unenclosed toilet, a sink, and a hot plate for cooking, often side by side.

Not surprisingly, such places are often filthy, smelly, stuffy, and hot. Insects and rodents scamper freely. Air circulation is poor, privacy is nonexistent, and personal hygiene is nearly impossible to maintain. There is usually no fire safety equipment of any sort. People who live in cage homes are often destitute, with no hope for a better future. As researchers have long known from working with lab mice, living year after year in such squalid, cramped quarters can lead to violence and a high incidence of mental illness.

Amazingly, the 16-square-foot (1.5 sq m) cages rent for around $170–$200 (USD) a month. Calculated by cost per square foot, these "homes" are more expensive than the most elegant apartments in Hong Kong.

Why does the government allow such conditions to exist? After all, government officials are well aware of the problem. In 2015, the Census and Statistics Department counted eighty-eight thousand such subdivided apartments, not including an estimated ten thousand it doesn't know about. If the hovels close down, more than two hundred thousand people would immediately be on the streets, homeless.

Bureaucracy and hidebound regulations also contribute to the problem. According to the Hong Kong Basic Law, new immigrants must wait seven years to become permanent residents. Meanwhile, until they receive a Hong Kong ID card, poor immigrants often have no choice but to live in bedspace apartments. And Hong Kong residents waiting for government-assisted housing must wait an average of four to six years, and sometimes longer.

Despite media coverage that has shocked the world, not much has been done to alleviate the misery of the poor in Hong Kong.

schools, hospitals, and commercial buildings around the apartment blocks.

The HKHA's long-term strategy is to produce new housing and to upgrade older estates to meet overwhelming demand, but change happens slowly in Hong Kong. As land on Hong Kong Island and Kowloon becomes even scarcer and more expensive, new urban centers, known as new towns, have sprung up in outlying areas. In some cases, abandoned factory buildings are remade into housing. Many people live on islands or in the New Territories and commute to work by ferry or train.

RICH AND POOR

In Hong Kong there is a stark contrast between the lifestyles of the rich and poor. The very rich dwell in palatial homes and employ a bevy of cooks, gardeners, chauffeurs, and other domestic servants. Many of the rich are Chinese people who have made money as factory owners, bankers, or merchants. The neighborhood of choice for the wealthy is Victoria Peak, located high above the city with magnificent views of the harbor.

Wealthy people can afford to live in the executive apartment buildings that surround Victoria Peak.

At the other end of the contrasting scale of lifestyles are homeless people who sleep under bridges or squatters who live in makeshift tents and cardboard homes at the edge of parks. Some of the older apartment blocks have deteriorated into virtual slums in which small apartments have been subdivided into many tiny units, sometimes even into boxes and cages, that people can barely fit into. A social security system is virtually nonexistent in Hong Kong.

WORKING LIFE

The life of most Hong Kong residents is dominated by work and the pursuit of money. Hong Kong's commercial beginnings, combined with its emphasis on free trade, have focused people's attention on economic activities. The shortage of farming land, the influx of refugees determined to survive and prosper, and the lack of a social security system all contribute to an atmosphere in which work and profit are the highest priorities.

To ensure economic security for themselves and their families, people work long hours and often take extra jobs. Being one's own boss is highly valued. Small businesses have mushroomed, from fruit stalls to fortune-tellers and roadside barbers. Some families work from home, taking on simple but monotonous manufacturing jobs, such as assembling toy parts. There are laws that prevent children under the age of fourteen from working in shops and factories, but in family businesses, even the children put in long hours to help the family survive.

On the streets of Hong Kong it seems as if everyone is always rushing to seal a business deal. Cell phones are a common sight as people conduct business on the run. Peddlers, executives in suits, and millionaires in limousines all wield the latest communication devices.

Farmers and fishermen have a slower, quieter life, but they are still industrious. Women perform hard work in the fields, chatting with one another as they sift the soil and pull up weeds. Their lifestyle has barely changed in hundreds of years. However, many of the men in rural areas now work in industries around towns, leaving the women to tend the farms.

Feng shui (fung shway), which means "wind and water," is a Chinese concept that most Hong Kongers take seriously. Feng shui is about living in harmony with the natural environment and tapping the goodness of nature to ensure good fortune and health. Hong Kong residents understand the importance of good feng shui—for them it is an essential ingredient for success.

Feng shui was first practiced in ancient China by farmers who believed that wind and water were important natural forces that had the power to either nurture or destroy their crops. The practice has developed into an art of positioning buildings and other structures, such as fountains, bridges, and graves, so that they exist in harmony with the surrounding environment. A specially designed compass measures the invisible forces that the Chinese believe exist beneath the earth. A balance of negative yin and positive yang forces in the immediate surroundings determines one's well-being.

Feng shui practitioners examine all aspects of a structure. When an existing building is involved, a feng shui master may suggest the best way to readjust the natural forces in order to create balance, perhaps by rearranging the furniture, repainting a room in a different color, or placing mirrors in front of doors to deflect negative energy. For a new building, a feng shui master's recommendations may range from site selection and building orientation to the alignment of doors and windows, as well as the placement of furniture.

WORKING MOTHERS Although Hong Kong is reputedly a great place to do business, it's not so great for business women—particularly working mothers of young children. Since 1995, statutory maternity leave in the territory has been ten weeks at 80 percent pay. That is certainly better than in some parts of the world, but a bit stingy by comparison to many industrialized nations. For example, Singapore provides sixteen weeks at full pay; Japan mandates fourteen weeks at two-thirds pay, plus childcare leave for each parent until the child turns one; and China itself provides fourteen weeks at full pay, or even higher. (The United States is unusual among wealthy nations in that it mandates no paid maternity leave at all, though employers may choose to offer it.)

A young boy blows a pinwheel at a Lunar New Year fair.

Hong Kong's working mothers also express concern about inflexible working hours and expensive childcare. And even for families that can afford high-priced child care, there are not enough facilities available. The city's pro-business atmosphere is not supportive of young families, many working mothers say. In a 2014 survey of working parents by the Hong Kong Society for the Protection of Children, 70 percent of the respondents cited the lack of affordable child care as a reason to forego having a second child.

Hong Kong spends 0.14 percent of GDP on the education and care of children under age six. By comparison, the European Union recommends governments spend 1 percent of GDP on young children.

EDUCATION

Education is a central tenet of Confucianism. Hong Kongers see education as the key to a better life for their children and for themselves, since parents expect their children to look after them in their old age. As a result proper education is a priority. Children spend long hours studying at school and at home. Competition to get into the best high schools and universities is fierce.

About 90 percent of Hong Kong students attend government-aided schools. Until 1971 even public elementary schools charged fees, but the government now provides nine years of free compulsory education for pupils up to the age of fifteen. Chinese is the language of instruction in most schools. English is taught as a second language. Private English-language schools and international schools are open to children of all races.

After going through compulsory junior high school (grades 7—10), students take central examinations and are allocated places for grades 11 and 12, according to their test results. They may attend grammar, technical, or prevocational schools.

Full-time higher education in Hong Kong consists of eight public universities, including the University of Hong Kong (which operates in the English language) and the Chinese University of Hong Kong (which operates

Students at La Salle Primary School work on computers in class.

in Chinese). There are also about a dozen private institutions of higher education. Those students whose families can afford it may choose to study overseas, often in Britain, the United States, or Canada. Many Hong Kong parents send their children abroad in the hope that the children can obtain permanent residence in these countries. This would enable their families to leave Hong Kong if they ever decide to stop living under Chinese administration in the future.

Hong Kong also has more than sixty special schools for students with visual, hearing, physical, emotional, and mental disabilities. The Ministry of Education tries as much as possible to integrate children with disabilities into the mainstream school system.

Being a cosmopolitan business hub, Hong Kong also has many private international schools to educate the children of expats, temporary foreign residents, and Hong Kongers who prefer a foreign language school. Tuition is typically very high at these schools, but the educational standards usually are as well, reflecting their culture of origin.

WEDDINGS

The actual marriage ceremony, which often takes place at the registry of marriages, is usually a simple affair, with only close family members and friends in attendance. The traditional wedding banquet, however, is produced on a much grander scale.

Wedding banquets in Hong Kong are a measure of one's status. The larger and more elaborate the banquet, the more "face" the bride and groom and their families will have. The result may be a sit-down dinner for hundreds of people in a huge ballroom. The other result of a huge wedding banquet is a huge bill. Traditionally the banquet is the financial responsibility of the groom's family, who treat the event as a celebration to welcome the future mother of their grandchildren. To help with the cost of the banquet, guests give *laisee* (ly-see)—red packets of lucky money—instead of gifts.

Wedding banquets are long, noisy affairs. The wedding meal usually has ten courses, which means that dinner lasts for two to three hours. Then there are the obligatory speeches. In the course of the evening, the bride will change from a Western-style white wedding gown into a traditional red outfit. The wedding couple walks from table to table to toast their guests and to receive lively toasts in return. When dessert is served, the party draws to an end. The couple and their parents see their guests off at the doorway.

The most important part of the traditional wedding is the tea ceremony. The new bride serves tea to all of her in-laws who are older than her husband. Referred to as *zham cha* (tsum chah), which literally means "serve tea," the ceremony is a way for the bride to show her respect to the elders in her new family. In ancient times this practice was used to judge the bride whom the groom had chosen. If his parents did not approve of the woman, they would not accept tea from the bride. Today family elders use the tea ceremony as an occasion to bestow their blessings on the couple.

FUNERALS

Like weddings, funerals in Hong Kong are an indicator of status. The more important and wealthy the deceased or the bereaved family is, the more people there will be at the funeral. When the funeral service begins, the casket is wheeled into the funeral hall. Mourners are expected to walk around the casket to pay their last respects.

If the deceased person was Christian, a Christian funeral service follows. If he or she was Buddhist or Daoist, the family holds a wake that may last for several days, with a priest burning incense and chanting prayers. To ensure that the deceased has sufficient money and other luxury items in the afterlife, paper money and paper models of consumer goods, such as houses, cars, and even servants, are burned. It is believed that when these paper images burn, the smoke carries them up to the heavens.

HEALTH CARE

Hong Kong residents enjoy good health due to extensive governmental implementation of community health services. The territory's low infant and maternal mortality rates are among the best in the world. Unfortunately Hong Kong's high population density means that it is occasionally susceptible to epidemics of major communicable diseases, such as avian flu and severe acute respiratory syndrome (SARS).

Hong Kong has forty-two public hospitals and eleven private hospitals. Established in 1990, the Hospital Authority runs hospitals and outpatient clinics, including maternal and child health centers. Mobile dispensaries serve villagers in remote areas of the New Territories, and islanders are visited by "floating clinics." Helicopters provide a "flying doctor" service to the more isolated and inaccessible communities.

Cases of tuberculosis, leprosy, and venereal disease are treated free of charge. Maternity and child health guidance, including prenatal services, postnatal care, and immunization, is also free. Free health-care services are available for children and adolescents at various stages of development. The elderly enjoy access to specialized health centers and medical care at little or no cost.

Despite the health-care system's successes, hospitals and clinics remain under great pressure, due to overcrowding. Patients often face a long wait for treatment.

INTERNET LINKS

http://www.dh.gov.hk/english/statistics/statistics_hs/files/Health_Statistics_pamphlet_E.pdf
This government pamphlet provides up-to-date health-related statistics for Hong Kong.

http://www.itseducation.asia/education-system.htm
This site provides an overview of education in Hong Kong.

https://www.theguardian.com/cities/gallery/2017/jun/07/boxed-life-inside-hong-kong-coffin-cubicles-cage-homes-in-pictures
This photo gallery exposes the shocking living conditions inside Hong's Kong's "bedspace apartments."

RELIGION

The Tian Tan Buddha is a huge monument and visitor attraction in Hong Kong.

8

MOST HONG KONG CHINESE practice a mix of Buddhism, Daoism, and Confucianism. Some people even combine these beliefs with Christianity. They go to church on Sunday and then visit a temple to burn joss sticks (incense sticks) for good luck. The practice of animism can still be found; offerings or joss sticks are placed at the foot of certain rocks and trees that are believed to house spirits. Hong Kongers are very tolerant of different religious beliefs.

Immigrants introduced Buddhism and Daoism to Hong Kong from mainland China. Some Buddhist and Daoist temples date back over seven centuries, while others were built in recent years with all the magnificence of traditional Chinese architecture. In all there are more than six hundred Buddhist and Daoist temples in the territory. There are also almost eight hundred Christian churches and chapels, a handful of mosques, Hindu and Sikh temples, as well as a Jewish synagogue.

BUDDHISM AND DAOISM

Prince Siddhartha Gautama founded Buddhism in India in the sixth century BCE. Disillusioned by the misery and injustice in the world,

The bronze Tian Tan Buddha, also known as Big Buddha, towers above the Po Lin Monastery on Hong Kong's Lantau Island. At 112 ft (34 m) tall, it is the largest seated bronze Buddha in the world—this Buddha sits peacefully upon a lotus flower. Visitors to the monument can climb the 268 steps to the base of the statue.

Confucianism is not a religion—or perhaps it is. Theologians and philosophers may debate the question and still not arrive at an answer. Either way, it is central to Chinese life, and Hong Kongers view Confucian ideas as important concepts. These guiding principles were passed down by Confucius (551–479 BCE), China's most famous and influential teacher and philosopher. Born at the time of the Warring States (403–221 BCE), Confucius taught a system of moral statecraft that would lead to peace, stability, and a just government. He is venerated as the man who established the code of conduct that forms the basis for much of Chinese culture and lifestyle.

Confucianism is a system of ethical precepts for the management of society based on the practice of sympathy, or "human-heartedness," which is demonstrated through a combination of etiquette and ritual. Confucius set out a code of behavior for five categories of loyal relationships: the relationship of a subject to a ruler, a son to his father, a younger brother to an elder brother, a wife to her husband, and a friend to another friend. Respect and loyalty, integral parts of any relationship, are fundamental Confucian values that strengthen social harmony.

Filial piety—respect and obedience to one's family elders—is another important Confucian value. Filial piety is a cohesive force that binds families together, even in Westernized Hong Kong.

Gautama renounced his royal heritage to seek enlightenment, which he attained after meditating for many years. After he became enlightened he was known as the Buddha. The term *Buddha* means "Enlightened One." The Buddha taught that the source of human suffering and misery springs from cravings and desires, and that meditating to eliminate desires can lead to spiritual enlightenment. Buddhism became established as a major religion in China in the sixth century CE.

Daoism (sometimes written as Taoism) originated in China around 2,500 years ago. Its founder was Laozi (sometimes spelled Lao-tzu), whose name means "Teacher" or "Old One." Daoism advocates a life of simplicity and passivity that follows the *dao* (*dow*, which rhymes with *how*)—the guiding path that leads to immortality. Many people who lived in harmony with nature, including Laozi, are now worshipped as Daoist gods.

Both Buddhism and Daoism were introduced to Hong Kong by Chinese immigrants, and the two religions' practices have merged to some extent. Almost every Buddhist and Daoist household has an ancestral shrine, and countless shops have a "God Shelf" that bears images of the owner's favorite deities. Traditional rites associated with birth, marriage, death, and festivals are still widely observed. Temples are especially crowded during festivals and on the first and fifteenth days of each lunar month. Although each temple is generally dedicated to one or occasionally two deities, it is common for the images of multiple deities to be displayed. Daoist priests perform elaborate rites, offering thanks to the gods or praying for prosperity and happiness.

Religious studies are conducted in monasteries, nunneries, and hermitages. Hong Kong's best-known monasteries are situated in more remote parts of the New Territories. The Buddhist Po Lin Monastery on Lantau Island is renowned for its view of the sunrise and its gigantic Buddha statue.

A golden statue of Laozi stands in the Hangu Pass Tourist Area of Lingbao in central China.

Hong Kong has always depended on the sea, first for fishing and then for trade. So it is not surprising that the territory's most popular deities are those associated with the sea and the weather. Tin Hau (also spelled Tianhou), the "Queen of Heaven" and protector of seafarers, is worshipped by an estimated 250,000 people. There are at least twenty-four Tin Hau temples in Hong Kong, with the earliest and most famous one at Fat Tong Mun in Joss House Bay.

Daoist and Buddhist organizations provide grants to meet welfare, educational, and medical needs in Hong Kong, either directly or indirectly via donations to assorted charities.

CHRISTIANITY

Christianity in Hong Kong dates back almost to the founding of the territory. The first church was established in 1841. Today more than seventy Protestant denominations exist, with at least 1,450 congregations, are practicing in Hong Kong. The Christian community numbers around 859,000—with about 480,000 of those being Protestants.

PROTESTANTS The Protestant community dates back to 1841. Baptists form the largest denomination, followed by Lutherans. Other major denominations include Adventists, Anglicans, and members of the Christian and Missionary Alliance, Church of Christ in China, Methodist, and Pentecostal churches. Due to their emphasis on youth work many congregations have a high proportion of young people. Since the 1970s the number of independent churches has increased significantly due to the evangelical zeal of lay Christians. Current membership numbers 320,000.

Protestant churches in Hong Kong are involved in education, health care, and social welfare. Protestant organizations operate three tertiary colleges and 630 schools that range from nursery school to secondary level. They also manage theological seminaries, Christian publishing houses, and bookshops. There are four Christian radio programs on Radio Television Hong Kong (RTHK). The Protestant movement also runs hospitals, clinics, and social service organizations. Their services include community and youth centers, day-care centers, children's homes, homes for the elderly, schools for the deaf, training centers for the mentally disabled, and camp sites.

The Saint Mary's Church in Wan Chai, Hong Kong, is a bit of an architectural oddity. The Anglican church was built in the 1930s as a cross between a Chinese temple and a Christian church.

CATHOLICS A Roman Catholic church was established in Hong Kong in 1841, and the territory became a diocese in 1946. There are about 379,000 Catholics in Hong Kong, in fifty-two parishes. Catholic services are usually conducted in Cantonese or Mandarin, with a few churches providing services in English.

In 1969 Francis Chen-peng Hsu became Hong Kong's first Chinese bishop. The present Bishop of Hong Kong (in 2017) is seventy-eight-year-old Cardinal John Tong Hon (b. 1939). One of the diocese's concerns is the community's well-being. As of 2016, the Catholic Board of Education administered 256 Catholic schools and kindergartens. Catholic churches provide medical and social services through the running of hospitals, clinics, social centers, hostels, homes for the elderly, and a home for the handicapped. These services are open to people of all faiths, and it is estimated that 95 percent of their beneficiaries are non-Catholics.

OTHER RELIGIONS

The Kowloon Masjid and Islamic Center in Tsim Sha Tsui serves the region's Muslim community.

ISLAM There are approximately three hundred thousand Muslims in Hong Kong. About fifty thousand of these are ethnic Chinese, while the rest hail from Indonesia, Pakistan, India, Malaysia, the Middle East, and Africa. There are three mosques on Hong Kong Island and one in Kowloon. The Shelley Street Masjid was the first to be built in Hong Kong, in the 1840s. The Kowloon Masjid and Islamic Center can accommodate about 3,500 worshippers.

The Incorporated Trustees of the Islamic Community Fund of Hong Kong coordinates all religious affairs, and manages mosques and Muslim cemeteries. The Chinese Muslim Cultural and Fraternal Association serves Chinese Muslims.

Charitable work among the Muslim community, such as financial aid to the needy, medical care, educational assistance, the provision of an Islamic kindergarten, and assistance for the aged, is conducted through various Muslim organizations in Hong Kong.

HINDUISM The religious and social activities of Hong Kong's strong Hindu community, which numbers one hundred thousand, are centered around the Hindu Temple in Hong Kong Island's Happy Valley district. The Hindu Association of Hong Kong is responsible for the upkeep of the temple, which is used for the observance of Hindu festivals, meditation, spiritual lectures, yoga classes, devotional music sessions, and other community activities. Naming, engagement, and marriage ceremonies are performed at the temple according to Hindu rites. Other important services rendered by the temple include the administration of last rites, cremation ceremonies, and the upkeep of the Hindu crematorium at Cape Collinson.

SIKHISM Hong Kong has a small Sikh community that numbers twelve thousand members. Established in 1901, a unique feature of the Sikh Temple is that it provides free meals and short-term accommodation for overseas visitors of any faith.

JUDAISM Hong Kong's small Jewish community worships at the Synagogue Ohel Leah, the Chabad Lubavitch, and several other locations. The synagogue was built in 1901 on land provided by Sir Jacob Sassoon and his family. The original site included a rabbi's residence and school, as well as a recreation club for the congregation, about four hundred member families. A Jewish cemetery adjoins the synagogue. The main worship site once housed a school and club, which have since been redeveloped into two residential blocks of apartments. The new Jewish Community Center offers both recreational and kosher dining facilities. It also has a specialist library devoted to all aspects of Judaism.

INTERNET LINKS

http://www.asiaatsea.com/tin-hau-chinese-goddess-of-the-sea
This well-illustrated article discusses Tin Hau and the sea-faring community of Hong Kong.

http://www.discoverhongkong.com/us/see-do/insiders-guide/traditions-and-spirituality/index.jsp
This travel site spotlights some of Hong Kong's top temples and sacred places.

https://www.gov.hk/en/about/abouthk/factsheets/docs/religion.pdf
This pdf government report provides an overview of religious groups in Hong Kong.

http://www.scmp.com/news/hong-kong/education-community/article/1866653/let-virtues-loyalty-and-decency-calm-restless
In this article from the *South China Post*, the president of the Confucian Academy discusses how Confucianism can benefit Hong Kong.

LANGUAGE

A bookshop in Hong Kong displays magazines and newspapers in English and Chinese.

9

THE LANGUAGE OF HONG KONG IS business," according to a rather droll observation. Money talks, to be sure, but Chinese is the main form of communication in Hong Kong, and English is widely spoken as well. Under the Official Languages Ordinance, enacted in 1974, both languages have equal status. Major reports and government publications are available in both English and Chinese versions. Simultaneous interpretation is provided at all government meetings. The civil service replies to correspondence from the public in either English or Chinese, depending on the language in which the initial correspondence is written. Since 1989 all new principal legislation is ratified in both languages.

When Britain returned Hong Kong to China in 1997, only about one quarter of the population spoke Mandarin Chinese, or Putonghoa, the language of mainland China. The majority spoke Cantonese Chinese. Twenty years later, about half of Hong Kongers can speak Mandarin, as relations between the two language worlds have become more intertwined. However, for political reasons, some Hong Kong folks flat out refuse to learn the mainland dialect.

Signs at the Hong Kong airport show Chinese characters and English.

To clarify, Chinese actually isn't actually a language at all—or at least not *one* language. Rather, it's a group of related, but often mutually unintelligible, language varieties. China is a huge country, and over the centuries many distinct Chinese dialects have developed. A speaker of one dialect may not understand a speaker from a different part of China. Written Chinese, however, is the same for all dialects. The commonly spoken dialect in Hong Kong is Cantonese, which is neighboring Guangdong province's predominant dialect.

Prior to 1974, English was Hong Kong's only official language, and knowledge of English has always been key to employment in the civil service and multinational corporations. This situation began to change, however, after Hong Kong reverted to Chinese administration. The government is now encouraging more proficient use of Chinese in the civil service. The ultimate objective is to develop a civil service that is proficient in Cantonese, Putonghua (the official language of China, commonly known as Mandarin), and English.

Non-Cantonese Hong Kongers usually speak their own language or dialect among themselves. However, almost all the people who have been born and raised in Hong Kong can speak Cantonese, regardless of their race.

SPOKEN CHINESE

With well over a billion speakers worldwide, Chinese is the most widely spoken language in the world. However, it requires time for the non-Chinese to grasp. The various tones are difficult to master, and the writing system is very complex.

Chinese has eight major dialects: Mandarin, Cantonese, Wu, Hakka (or *Kejia*), Xiang, Gan, northern Min, and southern Min.

Zhang (tseng) means "cool," "neat," "fine," or "excellent." It can apply to situations, people, or objects. You can have zhang cars, zhang clothes, and zhang books. When applied to people, it means that they are physically attractive. Ho zhang wo adds emphasis—meaning "really cool" or "excellent."

Yau mo gau cho (yow mo gow cho) literally means "Has something gotten messed up?" but can be interpreted as "Are you kidding me?" It's a good phrase to use when you are frustrated that things are not going your way.

Lei po (lay poh) means "ridiculous." To add frustration, you can say lei sai po (lay sy poh).

Although Cantonese originated in China's Guangdong province, Hong Kong's people have their own distinctive style of speech. Cantonese is the language of the streets, and it is also the prime language of Hong Kong's popular culture. Almost all of the territory's movies and songs are produced and performed in Cantonese.

In China, Mandarin is spoken by at least 70 percent of the Han people, who constitute more than 90 percent of the total population. The official language of China is based on the Mandarin that is spoken in Beijing and is known as Putonghua or "common speech." References to standard Chinese or simply to the Chinese language usually mean Putonghua.

Chinese is a tonal language. This means that the same syllable can have different meanings depending on the way it is pronounced. For example, by speaking in different tones (such as rising, falling, high, or low), the syllable *ma* can mean "mother," "numb," "horse," or "scold." Putonghua has four distinct tones, whereas Cantonese has nine, though some sources say the old tonal distinctions have blurred and modern Cantonese has only six tones.

Both Mandarin and Cantonese have an abundance of homonyms—words that sound the same but have different meanings—for example, in English, *meet* and *meat*. In Hong Kong, when a word sounds like something auspicious,

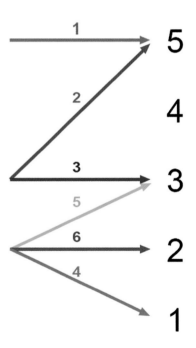

This graphical representation shows the six tones of Cantonese: 1, high-flat; 2, mid-rising; 3, mid-flat; 4, mid-falling; 5, low-rising; 6, low-flat.

Here are numbers one through ten and their approximate sounds in Cantonese.

一	*one.*	yuht
二	*two*	ngee (nee)
三	*three.*	sahm
四	*four*	sei (say)
五	*five.*	nmm (mm)
六	*six*	luhk
七	*seven*	tchat (tsat)
八	*eight.*	baat
九	*nine*	gau (gow)
十	*ten.*	sahp

it takes on a special significance. The word for "bat" is *fu*, which sounds like the word *fu*, meaning "good luck." Fish (*yu*) sounds like "plenty" (*yu*). As a result, bats and fish are considered lucky creatures, and they are featured in all sorts of designs and decorations. On the other hand, the number four (*sei*) is considered unlucky because it sounds like the word for "death" in Cantonese.

WRITTEN CHINESE

Although spoken Chinese dialects may differ enormously, all literate Chinese speakers can communicate with one another in writing, because all Chinese characters are written the same way, regardless of dialect. This makes it easier for the Chinese government to disseminate information about policies in Hong Kong. The government is able to reach Cantonese-speaking Hong Kongers in writing.

Written Chinese is based on ideograms. This means that each character is frequently a pictorial representation of an idea. For example, the Chinese character for "mountain" is represented by a simplified line drawing of a mountain. In the early stages of the language, one ideogram represented one word. As more words were gradually added to the language, two or more elements were combined to form a new ideogram. Sometimes two ideograms represent one idea. There are more than fifty thousand characters in written Chinese. Of these, about three thousand are in common use. The simplest character has only one stroke, while the most complicated has thirty. Not surprisingly, Chinese speakers consult a dictionary to look up characters they have not seen before or those that they have forgotten how to write.

Tightly packed signs hang across streets in the city.

The Chinese government introduced a simplified form of Chinese characters in 1964, because the writing system was so complicated. The simplified characters retain the basic shape and meaning of the original characters, but they have fewer strokes. Hong Kong, however, rejected the new characters and retains the traditional form.

LEARNING ENGLISH AND PUTONGHUA

Even though most high school students in Hong Kong study English as a first or second language, the general standard of spoken English is poor. Most Hong Kong Chinese think of English as a foreign language, and very few communicate in English outside the classroom. However, mastery of English is still viewed as an essential step toward getting a good job or emigrating. This translates into a reasonably high demand for English-language schools. There are also language schools that teach conversational English to adults who wish to improve their job prospects.

Many Hong Kong emigrants who have settled in English-speaking environments around the world will quickly realize that the English they learned in school is really a mix of English and Cantonese that is not very useful outside of Hong Kong. Many end up hiring a private tutor to help them communicate in their new place of residence.

ROMANIZATION

The Chinese languages don't use the Latin, or Roman, alphabet (A, B, C, etc.) in their written texts. In fact, they don't use an alphabet at all. Alphabets are made up of letters that stand for sounds. In Chinese writing, the symbols, or characters, represent meanings, not sounds. It's not that each word has its own character; rather, most Chinese words are written using two or more characters. Most literate Chinese people know and use between three thousand and four thousand characters. In Hong Kong, the list of traditional Chinese characters for use in schools contains 4,759 characters.

Translating Chinese dialects into the Roman alphabet—a process called romanization—involves converting the sounds of the spoken language into written words that Westerners can read. Various systems have been devised over the years to try to come as close as possible to approximating the right sounds.

The process is imperfect because there are sounds in Chinese that don't exist in English and vice versa. For example, most Chinese people cannot pronounce the V sound because it has no equivalent in Cantonese or Mandarin. Most will substitute a W or F sound, depending on the word.

The Yale system for the romanization of Cantonese was developed in 1958 specifically for American students learning Cantonese, so the pronunciation is based on American English. It remains widely used today. The Hong Kong Government has its own style of Cantonese romanization, and yet another system, called Jyutping, was created by the Linguistic Society of Hong Kong in 1993. There are also several other styles.

Another difficulty of all attempts at romanization is the problem of representing intonation. Spoken Chinese languages are tonal, meaning the rise or fall of the voice can change the meaning of the word. Representing tone is not a problem in written Chinese, because it is based on characters rather than letters. But in romanization, the sound of the word is represented in the written form. Various romanization systems use accent marks, diacritics, and numbers to represent tone.

In Hong Kong, the most commonly used romanization systems are Jyutping, and Cantonese Pinyin. Google Cantonese uses Yale, Jyutping, or Cantonese Pinyin, with Yale being the first standard.

Today Hong Kong residents have to learn Putonghua, the official language of China, in addition to English. Although the writing system is the same for Cantonese and Putonghua, the spoken language is completely different. Learning to speak it is supposedly as difficult as learning English. Putonghua is currently taught from the first year of primary school until the last year of secondary school.

MEDIA

Being the bustling, vibrant metropolis that it is, Hong Kong naturally has a wealth of media sources. It's a major center of broadcasting and publishing and has a very high rate of internet connection.

INTERNET At least 85 percent of Hong Kongers are online—more than six million—and they enjoy some of the world's fastest average internet connection speeds and free Wi-Fi is widely available. So far, there is very little internet censorship beyond the usual Western standards of protecting children and copyrighted materials, and banning computer crime. The Hong

Researcher Ma Chi Yuen demonstrates a speech-activated web browser that recognizes English, Mandarin, and Cantonese.

Despite the Basic Law's guarantee of "freedom of speech, of the press, and of publication," Hong Kong's media scene has been increasingly pressured into self-censorship. The People's Republic of China has a poor record when it comes to free speech. The media are not permitted to criticize the Communist Party, and journalists may be convicted of espionage and jailed for long periods, even for life, if they do not follow the government's line. The official Chinese news agency, Xinhua, has the right to censor news. Hong Kong's huge media industry, which was once said to be the freest in Asia, is struggling to maintain objective coverage in the face of increasing economic and political constraints.

In 2017, Freedom House, a nongovernmental organization which evaluates and ranks freedom of the press worldwide, downgraded Hong Kong's press freedom score to a 42 out of 100 (0=Most Free and 100=Least Free). This score put Hong Kong in the category of "Partly Free." The last time Hong Kong received a rating of "Free" was in 2008, with a score of 30, and its score has been dropping lower ever since. For its part, China scored 87 in the same 2017 ranking, placing it deep into the "Not Free" category for press freedom.

Freedom House reported, "Conditions for press freedom in Hong Kong have deteriorated over the last several years. Residents ... continue to enjoy much greater political rights and civil liberties than their counterparts on the mainland, including access to diverse news media and freedom from internet censorship. However, Hong Kong journalists have faced a growing risk of violence in the course of their work, and media independence is increasingly undermined by local authorities, pressure from Beijing, and the role of wealthy owners with political and business interests in mainland China."

Kong government respects freedom of expression and doesn't interfere with news and political websites. However, with increasing oversight from Beijing, which does censor internet within China itself, the future of internet freedom is uncertain.

TELEVISION Hong Kong has two television channels—one commercial station and one public channel. Cable and satellite networks offer hundreds of other channels which broadcast in English, Cantonese, Putonghua, and other languages. In addition, the privately-owned Phoenix Television broadcasts six channels to mainland China, Taiwan, and Hong Kong.

NEWSPAPERS AND MAGAZINES Hong Kong has a wealth of print publications, including Chinese-language dailies, English dailies, bilingual titles, and other language papers and magazines.

The Chinese-language dailies cover general news, both local and overseas. Top-selling papers include *Ming Pao*, *Ping Kuo Jih Pao* (*Apple Daily*), and *Tung Fang Jih Pao* (*Oriental Daily*). The last two specialize in entertainment, especially television and movie updates and horse racing. The larger papers are distributed to Chinese communities overseas. The *South China Morning Post* is the largest English language daily.

Periodicals also enjoy a booming business in Hong Kong. More than 600 publications are registered, over half of which are in Chinese. The numerous titles cover an extensive range of subjects, from current affairs to technical knowledge and entertainment guides.

Hong Kong is the Southeast Asian base of operations for many global and regional media. International news agencies such as the Associated Press are represented in the territory. International papers such as the *Wall Street Journal* have locally printed editions, as do international current affairs magazines such as *Time*. Regional magazines including *Asiaweek* and the *Far Eastern Economic Review* are also based in Hong Kong.

INTERNET LINKS

http://www.bbc.com/news/world-asia-china-40406429
This BBC article examines Cantonese and Mandarin usage in Hong Kong.

https://freedomhouse.org
Freedom House provides an up-to-date report each year on freedom of the press in Hong Kong, China, and other countries around the world.

http://www.omniglot.com/chinese/spoken.htm
Omniglot offers an introduction to the various versions of spoken Chinese, including a section on Cantonese, and also has links to information on written Chinese and related matters.

ARTS

Hong Kong Island, as seen from across the harbor from Kowloon, dazzles during the nightly light show.

10

FROM ANCIENT CHINESE ART FORMS to cutting-edge works that defy easy categorization, Hong Kong has something for the art lover in everyone. Its lively exhibition and performance scene attracts artists and art afficionados from around the globe.

Residents and visitors alike can enjoy hundreds of cultural events, from traditional Chinese opera, puppet shows, and classical music performances to Western ballet and theater. The Hong Kong Philharmonic Orchestra, the Hong Kong Chinese Orchestra, the Chung Ying Theater Company, and the City Contemporary Dance Company are among the best-known local artistic groups.

Art exhibitions showcase the works of local and international painters and sculptors. Hong Kong is a major center for the sale of Asian art and antiques. Hollywood Road in the Central District is crowded with antique and curio shops, while major auction houses such as Sotheby's and Christie's have offices in Hong Kong. The territory's entertainment industry is world renowned. Cantonese movies and music are increasingly exported beyond Asia to the rest of the world.

Each evening at 8 p.m., Hong Kong bursts into "A Symphony of Lights." This daily light and sound show has been noted as the largest such event by the Guinness World Records. The nightly spectacle involves interactive lights on forty-seven buildings around Victoria Harbor. Spectators can listen to the music and narration on the harbor front by way of radio or phone.

CALLIGRAPHY

The Chinese have developed calligraphy into an art form. In earlier centuries scholars had to master calligraphy in order to pass the all-important civil service examination, and great importance is still placed on good handwriting.

All that an artist requires for Chinese calligraphy is a brush, an ink stick, an ink stone, and paper. Calligraphers write poems, couplets, or proverbs. A well-written calligraphic piece plays on the senses, with the brush strokes invoking images of strength, beauty, or grace. Even if one cannot interpret what the characters mean, the piece still is appreciated for its aesthetic value.

There are several forms of calligraphy. The formal style has angular characters and few curved lines. Characters written in the "grass" style are more flowing and cursive. Only those who have studied Chinese calligraphy intensively can decipher characters that are written in this style.

A calligrapher brushes Chinese characters onto graph paper.

PAINTING

Traditional Chinese paintings are usually done on silk or absorbent paper. There are five categories of subjects: human figures, landscapes, flowers, birds and other animals, and fish and insects. A pointed brush is used for coloring. Some styles only use black paint, while others are more colorful.

Chinese artists do not paint with a model before them. They paint from the images in their memory. Their work is swift, and the brush strokes are confident. Once done the artist may paint the picture many times over until he or she achieves the desired effect. Chinese artists do not simply paint an image; they also attempt to capture the spirit in their creation. To that end artists sometimes spend hours meditating and concentrating before expressing their thoughts on the paper. Many artists are known to paint only certain subjects, such as horses or birds.

Artists are evaluated on their brush strokes. Brush strokes are given special names, and critics examine how the brush strokes contribute to the effect of the picture. Calligraphy in the form of a couplet or a short stanza of poetry is almost always used to complete a painting, as it is believed to complement the picture.

FINE ARTS

The Chinese are well known for their porcelain and ceramic artifacts. Vases, urns, bowls, and plates are adorned with symbols of nature, the seasons, or myths. Sometimes they are decorated with calligraphy. The best known is the Ming style of blue-and-white porcelain.

Cloisonné is another popular fine art. Cloisonné is a method of decorating metal surfaces with enamel. Metal pieces are attached to a base plate, forming sections that are filled in with enamel paint. When the piece is heated the enamel fuses to the metal, forming a glossy, colored surface. Although the art was introduced to China from the Middle East, the Chinese perfected the technique. Today cloisonné decorates everything from chairs to chopsticks.

The Chinese are also masters of carving. Jade, ivory, and rosewood are intricately carved. Sometimes knives as small as toothpicks are used for finer work. Carved rosewood furniture inlaid with intricate mother-of-pearl designs are popular items.

CHINESE OPERA

Chinese opera started out as street performances where gongs, cymbals, and drums were used to attract passersby. Even today a piece with these instruments would herald the beginning of a new opera scene. Opera plots are taken from historical tracts, folk legends, classical novels, and fairy tales. Opera includes a combination of many skills, such as singing, dramatic speech, acrobatics, and dancing. An orchestra of Chinese

The Chinese Cantonese Opera 2016 troupe performs in Tung Chung, Hong Kong.

fiddles, flutes, clappers, drums, cymbals, and gongs usually complements the action.

Chinese opera stages are usually quite bare and have few props. Chairs may represent hills. A flag with the character for "river" written on it represents a body of water. However, the lack of scenery is more than made up for by the intricately embroidered costumes and glittery headgear that the performers wear. Artists wear robes with long, wide sleeves. The sleeves are used for flirting and for depicting fear or anger. The actors' makeup is very heavy and elaborate, with different colors signifying different character traits, such as loyalty or intelligence. Gods and fairies are represented with gold or silver makeup. Yellow is the color of emperors, and green represents a person of high rank.

Operas usually last for several hours. The atmosphere is festive, and the action is not limited to the actors on stage. Spectators stand up and join in the chorus. Their loud comments in response to the stage action are often as entertaining as the opera itself. This art form is declining, as young Hong Kongers increasingly favor entertainment alternatives from the West.

CHINESE ORCHESTRAS

Traditional Chinese music is popular with Hong Kong's older population. The eighty-five-member Chinese Orchestra holds regular concerts at the Cultural Center and in other halls throughout the territory.

Traditional musical instruments include the *erhu* (ER-hoo), a two-stringed fiddle; the *yue chin* (YOO-eh chin), a four-stringed banjo; the *guzheng* (KOO-chuhng), zither; the *hu chin* (HOO chin), a two-stringed violin; and the *pipa* (PEE-pah), a four-stringed lute.

For the uninitiated traditional Chinese music may be difficult to appreciate. In order to appeal to a wider range of tastes, including Western audiences, the traditional instruments are being modified, or accompanied by Western instruments such as the cello, and are being used experimentally to perform modern compositions.

CANTOPOP

Hong Kong is the center of a thriving Cantonese pop music industry, commonly called "Cantopop" or "HK-pop." It is based on Western popular musical forms, rather than traditional Chinese music.

Cantopop stars have a huge following in Hong Kong, Taiwan, Singapore, and other Chinese-speaking communities. They also have many fans in Asian countries such as Japan. They are even popular among people who do not speak Cantonese. Many of the singers record songs in Putonghua, and some even record in Japanese.

Among the biggest Cantopop stars in the 1990s were four solo male singers whose popularity earned them the title of "Heavenly Kings"—Andy Lau, Aaron Kwok, Jacky Cheung, and Leon Lai. Now middle-aged men, each went on to have solo singing careers, with Lau and Lai becoming actors.

Major female stars include Faye Wong, Sandy Lam, and the pop duo Twins. Although these singers are virtually unknown outside of Asia, top performers, such as Jacky Cheung, have sold as many records as Michael Jackson or Madonna. Their publicity tours attract legions of loyal fans who range from prepubescent teens to working adults and retirees.

MOVIES

Hong Kong is the world's largest producer of Chinese-language action movies. The territory also exports movies all over Asia, even to non-Chinese-speaking countries. These days Hong Kong movies have gained a following in the United States. Many Hong Kong stars are now household names around the world. Here are some of them:

JACKIE CHAN (b. 1954), is the reigning king of action cinema, thanks to his comedy/martial arts movies. Having starred in the *Rush Hour* series, he is a familiar face to American audiences. Recently Chan received an MTV lifetime achievement award.

CHOW YUN-FAT (b. 1955), is one of Hong Kong's most prolific actors. Chow has acted in movies of every genre and was one of the stars in the internationally acclaimed *Crouching Tiger, Hidden Dragon*, directed by Academy Award—winning director Ang Lee. In 2014, Chow was the second-highest earning actor in Hong Kong.

BRUCE LEE (1940—1973), born Lee Sui Lung, remains a movie legend. He was probably the first Chinese martial arts actor to become a well-known figure in the West and a household name around Asia. His son Brandon followed in his footsteps. They both died mysteriously at a young age.

JOHN WOO (b. 1946), earned himself a place in film history by directing many Hong Kong action movies. He grabbed Hollywood's attention with films such as *Broken Arrow* and 1997's *Face Off* starring John Travolta and Nicolas Cage. His best-known works—*The Killer*, *Bullet in the Head*, and *Hard Boiled*—show characters struggling with questions of loyalty and honor. Woo's distinctive style is conveyed through elaborately choreographed action sequences. Film festivals, independent movie theaters, videotapes, and laser disks have earned him a legion of new fans.

WONG KAR-WAI (b. 1958) is a Hong Kong "Second Wave" filmmaker known for some of Hong Kong's most critically acclaimed movies. His productions are moody and atmospheric art films, including *Days of Being Wild* (1990), *Chungking Express* (1994), and what is often called his masterpiece, *In the Mood for Love* (2000).

Women in Hong Kong cinema are not relegated to soft roles. They are often central characters in kung fu or martial arts movies, wielding swords, performing acrobatics, and felling bad guys with the best of the men. Some of the better-known Hong Kong actresses are Maggie Cheung and Anita Yuen. Anita Mui, who was also a Cantopop diva dubbed "the Madonna of Asia," died in 2003 of cervical cancer.

INTERNET LINKS

http://artcentralhongkong.com
This new annual arts showcase focuses on Hong Kong's high-end contemporary art scene.

http://www.discoverhongkong.com/us/see-do/arts-performance/index.jsp
Museums, performance venues, and popular arts festivals are highlighted on this travel site.

https://www.timeout.com/hong-kong/film/best-hong-kong-movies
Timeout reviews its picks for the top 100 Hong Kong movies of all time.

http://www.tourism.gov.hk/symphony/eindex.html
This site for the "Symphony of Lights" includes a photo gallery.

LEISURE

Tourists sunbathe at the Stanley Town Beach in Hong Kong.

LEISURE? WHAT LEISURE? IT CAN seem as if the people of Hong Kong are always in a hurry, always working. People put in long hours at work, only to have a long commute home, depending on where they live. Schoolchildren don't have much leisure time either. After school there are activities, lessons, and homework until bedtime.

But fast-paced as life is, Hong Kongers do manage to enjoy themselves. Families picnic in the park, visit the outlying islands, take a trip to the amusement park, or swim and relax at the beach. Weekends are also a time for the family to dine out and perhaps indulge in special dishes that are too time-consuming to prepare at home. Movie theaters have local and foreign movies that cater to all tastes.

Those who prefer more active forms of leisure engage in different forms of sports, including golf, cricket, soccer, tennis, and squash. The Urban Council and other government organizations provide courts and sports grounds, roller-skating rinks, jogging tracks, children's playgrounds, camping grounds, beaches, swimming pool complexes, parks and gardens, aviaries, and a zoo. The wealthy enjoy pleasure boating, sailing, and waterskiing in Hong Kong's many inlets and bays.

The elderly, who have more leisure time, may spend time playing board games. The two most popular board games are Chinese chess and *weiqi* (way-chee). *Mah-jongg*, a game played with tiles, is also phenomenally popular. This is partly because it involves gambling, and for many Hong Kongers, gambling is a passion.

11

PARK OUTINGS

The fountain and flowers of the Hong Kong Zoological and Botanical Gardens create a peaceful haven in the city.

Contrary to the popular belief that Hong Kong is nothing more than a concrete cityscape, the territory actually has many parks scattered throughout its various regions. Its country park system covers 40 percent of the total land area.

Parks are important venues for leisure activities. Almost every day parks are full of people walking, exercising, or just relaxing. On weekdays parks are busiest in the early morning. This is when the young and old visit the park to exercise before going to work or school. Groups of people practice martial arts; children play games such as badminton; older men sit under the trees playing Chinese chess.

On Sundays parks are often converted into fair sites. The streets are cordoned off, crowds gather around the ice cream and soda stalls, and people from all walks of life enjoy free performances. Parks in more remote areas are ideal spots for kite flying, picnicking, hiking, cycling, and camping.

TAI CHI

Every morning Hong Kong is filled with people practicing tai chi. This Chinese martial art is primarily practiced for health. Tai chi emphasizes complete relaxation and is essentially a form of meditation; hence its nickname, "meditation in motion." Unlike conventional martial arts, tai chi is characterized by gentle, slow, flowing movements, which are precisely executed. Each action emphasizes force, rather than brute strength.

Tai chi traces its roots back to yoga, which was introduced to China from India. It gradually evolved into a Chinese martial art. In the thirteenth century a Daoist monk adapted the martial art into what has come to be known as tai chi. Over the centuries different styles evolved. The Yang style is the most common traditional form of tai chi practiced today.

The *chi* in the term *tai chi* refers to an ancient Chinese concept of energy. This energy, or chi, flows throughout the body, but it can become blocked, causing the body to become ill. There are several means of releasing the flow of chi. Two of the more commonly known methods are acupuncture and tai chi.

An older couple performs tai chi in a park.

In addition to its physical benefits, tai chi is believed to bring about certain psychological effects. As a form of meditation it can help people understand themselves and enable them to deal with others more effectively. Tai chi is based on the Daoist belief that there are two opposing principles in the universe: *yin* and *yang*. By restoring the balance of yin and yang through tai chi, people can improve their physical and spiritual well-being.

Although tai chi used to be practiced mainly by the elderly, it has now caught on with the younger generation, who view it as a means of relieving stress.

HONG KONG FLOWER SHOW

Each spring, Victoria Park bursts into bloom for the annual Hong Kong Flower Show. Produced by the Leisure and Cultural Services Department, the show is an extravagant display of horticultural beauty and creativity. Each year a different theme and theme flower provides focus—in 2017, the theme was "Blossoms of Love" and the flower was the rose. Music and dance performances,

floral art competitions, fashion shows, workshops, and discussions round out the ten-day experience. In 2017, more than 670,000 visitors attended and some 200 horticultural organizations from seventeen countries participated in the fragrant festival.

BEACHES AND POOLS

When the scorching summer heat strikes, swimming becomes Hong Kongers' recreation of choice. The government has designated forty-one beaches as safe spots for aquatic activities. However, beaches where sharks have been spotted are off limits. There are also forty-three public swimming pool complexes throughout Hong Kong Island, Kowloon, and the New Territories. Four of these are heated pools for winter use.

A must-visit vacation spot for both kids and adults is Ocean Park Hong Kong, also called Ocean Park. Located in Aberdeen on Hong Kong Island, it combines both an oceanarium and amusement park facilities. A range of rides, such as Ferris wheels and roller coasters, is available. Ocean Park also boasts the educational Dinosaur Discovery Trail, the Goldfish Pagoda, and the Butterfly House. Other attractions include a 738-foot (225-m) outdoor escalator, two aviaries, a bird theater, and a cultural village that teaches children about Chinese history, arts, crafts, mythology, customs, and inventions.

MAH-JONGG

Mah-jongg, an ancient Chinese game with many variations, is probably the number-one pastime in Hong Kong. A mah-jongg set of tiles is something like a deck of cards. There are 152 tiles, of which 108 are suit tiles (there are three suits). The rest are symbols and are generally more valuable than the suit tiles. The object of the game is to build sets of tiles.

Mah-jongg is a popular pastime.

Mah-jongg is a very lively game, with much clattering of tiles and friendly conversation. Four people are needed to play the game. The tiles are turned over and mixed up, or "washed." Each player then chooses a certain number of tiles. The players take turns to discard and pick up new tiles. The first player to build a complete set wins. There are very complicated rules governing how the sets can be built. Different types of sets command different points. The game can be played with or without gambling. Gambling comes in when the players agree on how much each point is worth before the game commences.

BOARD GAMES

In parks or in the common areas of public housing estates, one usually finds men seated on stools bending over board games. These men are playing Chinese chess or *weiqi* (also known as *go*), games that require a great deal of strategy.

Chinese chess traces its roots back to the eighth century. Chess pieces include elephants, cavalry, infantry, and a fortress where the king and his counselors are entrenched. The two halves of the board are separated by the Yellow River. The objective is to storm the opponent's fortress and capture the military commanders.

Weiqi has been around for thousands of years, and is the oldest board game in China. It is played on a grid of nineteen horizontal and nineteen

One of the newest Disneyland Resorts opened in Hong Kong in 2005. It was the second of three such parks in Asia—the others being Tokyo Disneyland in Japan, which opened in 1983; and the newest, Shanghai Disneyland on mainland China, which opened in 2016. (Outside of the United States, which is home to the original Disneyland in California and Walt Disney World in Florida, the only other international Disneyland Park is in Paris.)

The Hong Kong park is located on Lantau Island and covers 310 acres, with three hotels and a workforce of 7,300 multi-lingual "cast members" representing more than thirty nationalities. Modeled on the original Disneyland, it features seven themed lands and areas—Main Street, U.S.A.; Adventureland; Tomorrowland; Fantasyland; Toy Story Land; and the new Grizzly Gulch and Mystic Point. The centerpiece of the park is the Sleeping Beauty Castle.

Although Hong Kong Disneyland has been popular, its attendance figures have been lower than expected, growing from 4.6 million in 2009 to a high of 7.5 million in 2014. Attendance fell to 6.1 million after the 2016 opening of the Disney park in Shanghai.

One of the early controversies involving the Hong Kong park involved shark fin soup. Considered a Chinese delicacy, the soup is opposed by animal rights activists as harmful to shark populations and cruel to the animals themselves. At first, the park planned to serve the soup at its wedding banquets, as is customary in Chinese tradition. But after sustained pressure from environmental groups and schoolchildren, Disney officials banned the soup outright.

vertical lines. The pieces consist of 181 black and 180 white flat, round counters. The object of the game is to capture the opponent's counters and territory. Because of the high number of possible moves, *weiqi* is considered the most complicated board game in the world.

HORSE RACING

Scores of Hong Kong Chinese love to gamble on horse races. When the races are under way at Happy Valley, many people take leave from work to attend, hoping to strike it rich. Hong Kong residents take note of race times and dates so that they know when to avoid the masses of traffic that head to and from the racetrack.

Horse racing is organized by the Hong Kong Jockey Club, which also operates lotteries.

INTERNET LINKS

http://www.discoverhongkong.com/us/see-do/highlight-attractions/top-10/index.jsp
Hong Kong's Top Ten Attractions, including Hong Kong Disneyland, are spotlighted on this travel site.

https://www.gov.hk/en/residents/culture/recreation/index.htm
The Hong Kong government site offers information about recreation options.

http://www.lcsd.gov.hk/en/hkfs/2017/index.html
The Leisure and Cultural Services site provides information and many photos of the Hong Kong Flower Show.

FESTIVALS

Traditional Chinese lanterns light up a celebration of the Mid-Autumn Festival, also known as the Moon Festival.

12

LIKE MOST PLACES IN THE WORLD, Hong Kong operates on the Western calendar, January through December, for day-to-day life. Thanks to its history as a British colony, it also incorporates some Western celebrations into its annual rotation of observances and public holidays. For the most part, however, Chinese tradition dominates the yearly festivities.

Chinese festivals in Hong Kong follow the Chinese calendar, which is lunar (based on the moon). The starting dates of each month vary from year to year, according to the phases of the moon. This is why some of the traditional holidays occur on different dates of the Western calendar each year.

The Lunar New Year is the most important festival in Hong Kong. Other important Chinese celebrations include the Ching Ming Festival in the spring, the Dragon Boat Festival in early summer, the Festival of Hungry Ghosts, and the Mid-Autumn Festival. These events are thousands of years old and are celebrated by Chinese people all over the world.

For its resident Christians, as well as tourists, Hong Kong puts on spectacular Christmas displays and events. Light shows, ballet and symphony performances, and grandly decorated shopping malls celebrate the season, while local churches present religious services, carol sings, and other special events.

The Chinese calendar moves in a twelve-year cycle. Each of the twelve years represents the temperament of twelve symbolic animals. These animals are also assigned to months, days, and hours, where they represent a person's "inner," "true," and "secret" animals, according to his or her month, day, and hour of birth. Each animal, in turn, is associated with its own element—metal, wood, earth, water, or fire. The combination of elements is said to determine a person's personality.

According to one of the system's many origin legends, the Buddha summoned all the animals of the kingdom when he was dying. The first twelve to arrive had years assigned to them. Historically, the Chinese astrological system dates to at least the Han Dynasty (second century BCE to second century CE) and probably several centuries earlier.

The ancient Chinese astrological system on which the so-called zodiac is based is far more complex than most popular culture references describe (including the list below), and is also subject to translation difficulties (including the culturally inaccurate word zodiac itself).

Year of birth	*Personality attributes*
Rat (1972, 1984, 1996, 2008)	*Charming, smart, creative, thrifty*
Ox (1973, 1985, 1997, 2009)	*Steadfast, methodical, reliable*
Tiger (1974, 1986, 1998, 2010)	*Dynamic, warm, sincere*
Rabbit (1975, 1987, 1999, 2011)	*Humble, artistic, clear-sighted*
Dragon (1976, 1988, 2000, 2012)	*Flamboyant, imaginative, lucky*
Snake (1977, 1989, 2001, 2013)	*Discreet, sensual, refined, intelligent*
Horse (1978, 1990, 2002, 2014)	*Sociable, competitive, adamant*
Sheep (1979, 1991, 2003, 2015)	*Artistic, fastidious, weak-willed*
Monkey (1980, 1992, 2004, 2016)	*Witty, popular, versatile, good-humored*
Rooster (1981, 1993, 2005, 2017)	*Aggressive, alert, perfectionistic*
Dog (1982, 1994, 2006, 2018)	*Honest, traditional, sympathetic*
Pig (1983, 1995, 2007, 2019)	*Caring, diligent, home loving*

CHINESE NEW YEAR

The first day of the first lunar month is the Chinese New Year, the most important festival for Hong Kong Chinese. It falls in late January or February. Because it marks the start of the year, every care is taken to ensure good fortune for the coming twelve months. Buildings are decorated and streets are strung with elaborate light displays. A huge fireworks display lights up Victoria Harbor, usually on the second day of the festival. Lion dances and other celebrations can be seen at hotels and in various residential areas.

The traditional Chinese lion is a good-luck symbol for the lunar new year.

Preparations usually begin with a thorough spring-cleaning. The home is decorated with good-luck symbols, such as bushes laden with kumquats (tiny oranges) —the Chinese word for "kumquats" sounds like the words for "gold" and "luck." People buy new clothes, fill rice bins and larders to the brim, mend quarrels, and repay debts.

The day before the Lunar New Year is the Kitchen God's Day. The Kitchen God judges the family's behavior and travels to heaven to make a report to the Jade Emperor. The picture of the Kitchen God is taken down and ceremonially burned outside the kitchen to send him on his way. Before he leaves he is worshipped with incense and candles. He is served a delicious meal of glutinous rice, honey, or sugar, and sometimes wine as well. These foods are smeared all over his mouth to make sure that what he says will be sweet and flattering.

The reunion dinner on New Year's Eve is significant. No matter how far from home people are, many travel back to dine with their parents. Certain preparations are traditional—raw fish symbolizes prosperity, while the New Year's cake made from rice flour represents unity. At midnight all the house lights are turned on to dispel bad luck that may be lurking in dark corners. Crowds pack the temples to offer prayers for prosperity in the coming year.

On New Year's Day everyone dresses up in new clothes to visit relatives and friends, and children receive *laisee*. People greet one another by saying *kung hay fat choy*, which means "wishing you prosperity." On this day, no work—not even housework—is done, in case good luck might be inadvertently chased away. Use of knives and scissors is avoided. Even falling down is considered a bad omen.

In some villages of the New Territories, lanterns are hung in ancestral halls during the Chinese New Year. Any local family that had a son born during the past year brings a lantern to the hall, and the men of the family gather to enjoy a special meal. It's a time of community-wide celebration.

FESTIVAL OF TIN HAU

Tin Hau, Queen of Heaven and Goddess of the Sea, enjoys a soft spot in the Hong Konger's heart. Legend has it that Tin Hau was once a mortal. She was born long ago on the twenty-third day of the third lunar month. Shortly before her birth, a red light was seen descending upon the house of her father, a poor fisherman.

One day, Tin Hau dreamed of her father and two brothers on their fishing *junks*, or boats, in a storm. In her dream, she grabbed the rigging and started to pull them ashore. At that moment her mother woke Tin Hau, causing her to let go of one of the ropes. When her brothers returned they told how a beautiful girl had walked across the raging waters and had dragged their junk to safety but said that she had been unable to save their father.

After Tin Hau's death, sailors began to tell stories of her appearing during storms and rescuing them from certain death. The red light that appeared at the time of her birth was seen upon masts. Viewed as a sign of Tin Hau's protection, it was called "Our Mother's Fire."

Today almost every Hong Kong ship carries her image, and dozens of temples in Hong Kong are dedicated to her. On her birthday in the spring, fishermen decorate their boats and gather at her temples to pray for good catches during the coming year.

CHING MING

In April, on the 106th day after the winter solstice, families visit cemeteries to sweep their ancestors' graves, repaint the inscriptions on the headstones, and show their respect. This festival is called *Ching Ming*, which means "Clear and Bright," and is also referred to as Tomb Sweeping Day. In observance, people light incense sticks and red candles on the graves. They set out rice, wine, tea, and other foods, and burn paper clothing and *spirit money*, which will symbolically drift to their dead ancestors with the smoke. The whole family kneels to pay their respects. Before they leave, they tuck several pieces of offering paper under a stone on top of the grave. This is a sign that the grave has been tended for another year.

Despite its solemn origins, Ching Ming rites have the atmosphere of a picnic because the family members eat the food offerings. The festival is a happy occasion when families get together to remember their ancestors.

Performers dance during a Tin Hau Festival in April 2016.

THE BUN FESTIVAL

The Bun Festival, which is unique to Hong Kong, takes place on the island of Cheung Chau, usually in May. The central attractions are three 60-foot (18-m) towers studded with pink and white buns. The buns are an offering to the ghosts of the islanders who, according to stories, were killed by a plague or by pirates.

During the four days of celebration religious observances, processions, and Chinese opera performances take place. On the third day people dressed in colorful costumes march, walk on stilts, or ride on floats through the winding streets of the village. At the end of the festival, after the ghosts have had their fill, the buns are distributed to the crowds.

THE DRAGON BOAT FESTIVAL

A dragon boat team competes in a race at Chai Wan Bay.

The Dragon Boat Festival in the fifth lunar month combines a traditional celebration with the exciting pace of a sporting event. It takes place in June around the time of the summer solstice.

It originated with the story of Qu Yuan (c. 340—278 BCE), a famous poet and royal minister who threw himself into a river when his king fell under the influence of corrupt officials and refused to heed Qu Yuan's wise advice. When the people realized what he had done, they raced out in their boats to save him or retrieve his body. When they couldn't find him, they threw rice into the water, hoping that the fish would eat the rice and spare his body. The dragon boats race every year as if they are looking for Qu Yuan's body, and everybody eats dumplings filled with meat and sticky rice wrapped in leaves.

The rowers sit two abreast in the long, narrow body of the dragon. The boats' heads and tails are dismantled and kept in local temples when they are not in use. New heads must be dedicated in a ceremony that involves painting each eye with a dot of vermilion paint mixed with blood from the comb of a brown chicken. Once this is done the dragon is "alive" and has to be treated with respect, presented with candles and incense, and protected from anything that might harm it.

HUNGRY GHOSTS

The Chinese believe that enormous numbers of ghosts roam the world. People may become ghosts if all their descendants die out, if they are murdered or commit suicide, or if they are unable to reach the afterworld because they did not have a proper funeral. The seventh lunar month is considered by the Chinese to be especially dangerous because that is when the gates of hell open, allowing ghosts to roam wherever they like. The gates of heaven are also thought to be unlocked, allowing happy spirits to visit their families for feasting and entertainment. Therefore it is necessary to placate wandering spirits by offering gifts of food and entertaining them with opera.

On the fifteenth day of the seventh month, typically in August or early September, people celebrate Yu Luan, or the Hungry Ghost Festival. This is the time to appease the ghosts and pay tribute to their ancestors. Opera performances take place on temporary bamboo stages, presented for the enjoyment of both the living and the dead. Worshippers can pray at special altars set up around the city, where huge sticks of incense burn night and day. People offer foods to hungry spirits, who are thought to be starving in the underworld.

Believers also perform their own ceremonies during the month-long festival. Besides offering food, the people also burn paper clothing and spirit money to appease the hungry ghosts.

On the harbor, decorated boats take offerings to ghosts who died at sea. While Buddhist monks or Daoist priests chant their liturgies on the boat, believers scatter rice upon the water and launch paper boats that are filled with gifts.

THE MID-AUTUMN FESTIVAL

The fifteenth day of the eighth lunar month is when the full moon shines brightest. This is also the time of the Mid-Autumn Festival. On this night, children carry lanterns and look for Chang Er, the lady in the moon. According to legend, Chang Er had a tyrannical husband who obtained a potion that would make him immortal. Fearing for the well-being of her people, Chang Er drank the potion instead and flew to the moon.

Traditionally families set up a table facing the moon and serve dishes with round foods such as apples, oranges, peaches, and *mooncakes*, which are pastries filled with sweet, mashed lotus paste. Besides symbolizing goodwill, these small pastries were also responsible for ending the Mongol-controlled Yuan Dynasty (1271—1368). Chinese rebels stuffed each mooncake with a note informing supporters about their rebellion date—the fifteenth day of the eighth lunar month. Today, rice, wine, and tea are offered together with paper clothing and spirit money made of gold and silver paper. Shops sell special decorations and brightly colored lanterns. Today battery-operated plastic lanterns made in the shape of military tanks or Mickey Mouse are common.

TA CHIU

In addition to lesser gods and ghosts, Daoists believe in three great spirits—the Three Pure Ones. These pure spirits live in the stars, at the true source of life, and they are beyond the reach of change or decay.

The aim of Ta Chiu, a Daoist festival of peace and renewal celebrated on December 27, is to invite the Three Pure Ones down so that they will wipe away evil, restore peace and harmony, and renew life for entire village populations. Ordinary villagers leave the rituals to the Daoist priests. They are content to make offerings to their own patron gods, renounce evil, do good deeds, and feed the hungry ghosts.

The Ta Chiu ceremonies are carried out on several levels. Daoist priests perform a ceremony for the Three Pure Ones in the temple. Operas are staged, and offerings are brought to the patron deities, whose images have been brought out of the temple to a temporary shrine for the occasion. Birds and fishes are liberated as a symbolic life-giving gesture. Cleansing the altar, ritual bathing, fasting, and the disposal of items, which the priests collect and burn in a large paper boat, signifies purification.

Finally there are two spectacular closing ceremonies. The priests read the names of all the villagers from a huge list. After that they send the list to heaven by burning it on the back of a paper horse, before posting a red paper duplicate list on the wall for everyone to see.

At midnight on the last day they preside over an enormous "clothes burning" session at which ghosts are fed, clothed, given money, and sent away. All the villagers eat a communal meal where the meat of the "golden pigs"—part of the offering to the gods—is looked upon as the most honored dish.

PUBLIC HOLIDAYS

Hong Kong has seventeen public holidays. Among these are New Year's Day (January 1), Easter (March or April), Ching Ming (April), the Dragon Boat Festival (June), the Mid-Autumn Festival (September), and Christmas Day (December 25). Chinese New Year is a three-day public holiday in either January or February.

Some public holidays have changed since Hong Kong became a Special Administrative Region of China. Festivals according to the British calendar have been eliminated, and new festivals have been introduced. For example, the Queen's birthday, which used to be marked with two public holidays in June, is no longer celebrated. New holidays include October 1 and 2, which celebrate China's National Day.

INTERNET LINKS

http://www.discoverhongkong.com/us/see-do/events-festivals/chinese-festivals/index.jsp
This Hong Kong guide gives information on the many Chinese festivals celebrated there.

http://www.scmp.com/magazines/post-magazine/article/1805140/how-hong-kong-has-made-tin-hau-festival-its-own
This article explains the history of Tin Hau worship and her festival today.

http://www.telegraph.co.uk/news/2017/05/30/dragon-boat-festival-hong-kong-harbour-pictures
A captioned photo gallery of Hong Kong's Dragon Boat Festival is presented on this news site.

https://www.timeanddate.com/holidays/hong-kong
This site lists the yearly holidays and observances in Hong Kong.

FOOD

Exquisitely decorated moon cakes are seasonal treats for the Mid-Autumn Festival.

13

FROM STINKY TOFU TO SNAKE SOUP to fried chicken feet to fish balls, Hong Kong's most iconic and beloved foods are not usually found in most Western Chinese restaurants. Hong Kong's food culture reflects the richness of China's culinary arts, as well as some fusion Chinese-Western dishes. Hong Kong-style French toast is one example, though it's considerably more Western than Chinese in origin. A double-decker white bread sandwich is spread with peanut butter or coconut jam, dipped in an egg batter and then fried in butter. Like French toast anywhere, it's served with syrup and butter.

Being a hub of international business, Hong Kong also features foods from cultures all over the world. Pizza and cheeseburgers are as available as is sweet and sour pork, which is a genuine Hong Kong favorite.

Family meals are not quite the same as restaurant offerings. A typical Hong Kong meal begins with tea. An appetizer, such as cold cuts of meat, follows. The main dishes follow next. There can be as many

Cantonese cuisine is popular in Hong Kong and is representative of what Westerners think of as Chinese food. An old Chinese saying indicates that cuisine from Guangzhou (Canton) is highly regarded—"To be born in Suzhou, to live in Hangzhou, to eat in Guangzhou, and to die in Liuzhou."

as ten courses for a formal dinner such as a wedding banquet. For a more ordinary family meal there may be three or four dishes of meat and vegetables, plus a soup, followed by dessert.

CANTONESE CUISINE

Because most Hong Kong Chinese originated in the area around Guangzhou (Canton), Cantonese cooking is by far the most popular cuisine in Hong Kong. This is what most people abroad know as Chinese food. Part of the reason for Cantonese cuisine's popularity is the way it is prepared. The food is light, cooked in a little water or oil, usually in a wok, and the process is quick. This seals in and preserves the flavors in the food.

Char sui pork has a sticky glaze.

Cantonese cuisine is known for its fresh, delicate flavors. Ingredients are prepared the same day and cooked just before serving. Seafood is so fresh, it hardly touches dry land before landing on the dinner table. In many seafood restaurants, customers can actually choose the live fish they wish to eat from tanks in which they are displayed. Chinese kitchens do not usually stock frozen and processed foods, although dried seafoods, such as shark's fin, shrimp, and abalone, are important ingredients.

Many dishes, especially vegetables and fish, are steamed. This avoids overcooking and preserves the delicate flavors of the food. The use of hot and spicy sauces is not common in Cantonese cuisine. Sauces are used to enhance flavors, not overpower them. They usually contain ingredients with contrasting flavors, such as vinegar and sugar, or ginger and onion.

Barbecued meats—especially a type of sweet barbecued pork called *char siu* (chah syoo) and barbecued goose called *siu ngor* (syoo gnaw)—are some Hong Kong favorites. Other popular Cantonese dishes include shark's fin soup; crabs, steamed or cooked in black bean sauce; congee, a thick Cantonese rice porridge; and the ubiquitous dim sum, small dishes, including fried or steamed stuffed dumplings in a wide variety of shapes and fillings.

DIM SUM

Dating from the tenth century, dim sum commands a special place in Cantonese cuisine. Dim sum literally means "to touch the heart." These bite-sized morsels of food are served in many Hong Kong restaurants, and their range is mind-boggling. You can choose from steamed or fried dumplings filled with meat or seafood, Chinese buns stuffed with sweet bean paste, spring rolls, chicken's feet, rice wrapped in leaves, and stuffed bean curd.

Dim sum forms part of the Chinese tradition of yum cha (Cantonese for "drinking tea"). It originated from the need to eat something during yum cha, when friends and colleagues would get together to discuss everything from business to family gossip. At a yum cha restaurant, the guests drink tea and choose dishes of dim sum from trays or bamboo baskets that are wheeled around.

There is an interesting tradition associated with yum cha. Instead of saying "thank you" when receiving tea, people sometimes tap the table twice with the knuckles of two fingers. Legend has it that a Chinese emperor traveled south disguised as an ordinary citizen, accompanied by his bodyguards. One day, in a teahouse, the emperor himself poured tea for one of his bodyguards. Instead of kneeling and bowing, which would have given away his emperor's identity, the bodyguard knocked on the table with two knuckles so that his fingers resembled kneeling legs. This gesture of respect gave rise to a tradition that is still practiced today.

YIN AND YANG FOOD

The Chinese believe that all food falls into three basic categories: Yang (or "heating") food warms the blood and reduces vital energy. Yin (or "cooling") food cools the blood and increases vital energy. Neutral food is balanced, and does not affect energy. Examples of yang food include fried items, lamb, mutton, chocolate, almonds, mangoes, and potato chips. Melons, apples, yogurt, pork, celery, salt, and bananas are all yin foods.

A vendor displays fresh vegetables at an outdoor market on Temple Street in Hong Kong.

Winter is the time for yang food, because the blood needs to be heated, and summer is the time for yin food. When ordering food in restaurants, the Hong Kong Chinese try to maintain a balance between yin and yang. Fried yang food may be teamed with steamed yin dishes, and "heating" meat dishes can be eaten along with some cooling vegetable dishes.

DRINKS

Common nonalcoholic drinks in Hong Kong include soft drinks, many varieties of Chinese tea, and local specialties such as soya bean drinks. Fruit smoothies usually come with green or red beans, fruit pieces, and black grass jelly. Milk or ice cream is sometimes added.

Some Chinese drink Western wine, but it is more common to find local beer and spirits on the dining table. Chinese wine is often rice-based and distilled. Cognac is a popular drink, especially for entertaining favored guests. Like the exotic dishes served in restaurants, its cost is designed to impress. Brands such as Remy Martin and Courvoisier are consumed like water. Hong Kong is one of the world's biggest cognac consumers.

A popular delicacy in Chinese culture, shark fin soup is a traditional part of a wedding banquet, and other special occasion meals. The soup is a symbol of high status. Serving it reflects upon the generosity of the host and conveys respect upon the guest.

The soup, essentially a whole or shredded shark fin floating in a thickened chicken and ham broth, varies in price depending on which kind of shark species is used. Some dishes reportedly cost upwards of $2,000 a bowl! The shark itself lends no flavor or nutrition to the dish—though the Chinese believe it has medicinal value—it is mainly symbolic. Mostly it is a treasured tradition, which is why it's hard to convince many Chinese to give it up.

Animal activists, like the people at the Hong Kong Shark Foundation, are trying to do just that. The demand for fins has decimated species like the silky, oceanic whitetip, and dusky sharks around the world. The process of finning itself is considered cruel—fishermen slice off the shark's fin while it is alive, and throw the animal back into the ocean to die slowly, unable to swim. Conservationists liken the process to killing elephants and rhinos for their tusks.

Many environmental organizations have campaigned for years to ban shark fins, with some success, but not much. In the United States, the Shark Finning Prohibition Act of 2000 and the 2011 Shark Conservation Act, have outlawed finning and the importation of shark fins. In Hong Kong, however, the delicacy continues to be widely available. Although some eating places, including Disneyland Hong Kong, have removed it from their menus, a 2015 survey by the Hong Kong Shark Foundation found that 98 percent of Chinese restaurants there still serve it.

Fried chicken feet are for sale at a farmers' market in Hong Kong.

EXOTIC FOODS

The Cantonese are well known for what some consider their bizarre taste in meat. The Hong Kong Chinese are no exception. They believe that the more exotic the meat, the more salubrious, or wholesome, its effects on the health. Snake is boiled into a thick soup, as are shark's fins. Sea slugs, crocodiles, and sundry other creatures are prepared in a variety of ways. Frog's legs fried with ginger and scallions are thought to strengthen one's legs. Bird's nest soup is made from the dried mucus of the swift's salivary gland, which it uses to line its nest. Some Chinese delicacies, such as bear's paws, are banned in Hong Kong.

TABLE ETIQUETTE

There is strict etiquette when eating with chopsticks. One must never use chopsticks to drum on the table, and it is most disrespectful to point them at another person or use them to gesture. When not in use chopsticks should be placed flat, not left standing vertically in a bowl, as the latter resembles incense offerings to the dead. Sometimes, for the sake of hygiene, diners will turn their chopsticks around and use the reverse end to take food from the serving dishes.

At mealtimes, whether at home or in a restaurant, it is customary to wait for everyone to be seated before beginning the meal. Children generally invite their elders to begin before helping themselves.

Large Chinese dining tables in Hong Kong usually have a rotating platform in the center called a lazy susan, on which the serving dishes are placed. Diners help themselves to a morsel of the dish in front of them, and then rotate the lazy susan, sampling each dish along the way. Food should be taken from the top of the plate. It is considered rude to dig around for a morsel of food. The choice morsels should also be avoided. They should be offered to the elders at the table or to honored guests. A good host will always tend to his or her guests and urge them to eat their fill.

The Chinese do not pour soy sauce on their rice, because this would swamp the subtle flavors of the meal. Instead the sauce is placed in a small side dish.

Hong Kongers do not linger at the table. When the last course has been served and eaten, the meal is over.

INTERNET LINKS

https://www.chinahighlights.com/hong-kong/food-restaurant.htm
This travel site suggests some famous Hong Kong dishes that might appeal to Westerners.

http://www.cnn.com/travel/article/best-hong-kong-dim-sum/index.html
This article reviews Hong Kong's best dim sum restaurants, with photos and interesting descriptions.

http://www.cnn.com/travel/article/hong-kong-food-dishes/index.html
A long list of intriguing foods are pictured and explained on this site.

http://hksharkfoundation.org
The Hong Kong Shark Foundation provides information and news about shark finning.

http://www.seriouseats.com/2011/04/guide-to-dim-sum-dumplings-siu-mai-bao-chinese-steamed-buns.html
This food site offers a quick ove rview of dim sum and restaurant etiquette.

YANGZHOU FRIED RICE

Serves: 2 or 3

1 cup (7 ounces/200 grams) dry white rice

3 tablespoons oil

2 large eggs, beaten

4 ounces (about 115 g) fresh shrimp, deveined
  and shells removed

1 each medium onion and carrot,
  peeled and diced

½ cup (about 4 oz/115 g) ham, cut into cubes

½ cup (about 4 oz/115 g) Chinese roast pork,
  sliced or cubed

½ cup frozen peas (about 125 g), no need to thaw

1 ½ teaspoons salt

1 Tbsp each soy sauce and Shaoxing wine or dry sherry

4 scallions, chopped

¼ tsp ground white pepper

Cook the rice according to the directions on the package. Spread cooked rice on baking sheet to cool and dry. (Rice can be made in advance and refrigerated.)

Beat eggs in small bowl and set aside. Heat the wok over medium high heat, and add 1 tablespoon of oil, followed by the beaten eggs. Fold and scramble them gently, taking care not to scorch the eggs. Transfer the eggs back into the bowl and set aside.

Increase wok to high heat. Add 2 tablespoons of oil and quickly stir fry shrimp until just pink. Remove and set aside. Stir fry the diced onion and carrot until slightly tender. Next, add the diced ham and pork, and stir-fry for 30 seconds.

Add the rice and stir-fry for 2 minutes, being sure to heat the rice uniformly. Add the salt, soy sauce, wine, shrimp and peas, and stir fry continuously for another 2 minutes until the rice is heated through.

Finally, stir in the scrambled eggs, scallions, and white pepper.

MANGO PUDDING

2 ½ cups (595 mL) cold water
1 ¼ cups (300 g) granulated sugar
1 pound (450 g) frozen or fresh mango chunks
2 (¼-oz/7 g) packets unflavored gelatin
½ tsp kosher salt
1 cup (240 mL) heavy cream, chilled
1 tsp freshly squeezed lime juice

Place 8 (6-oz/180 mL) ramekins on a baking sheet; set aside.

Place ¾ cup (180 mL) of the water and ½ cup (120 mL) of the sugar in a small saucepan over high heat. Stir until sugar is dissolved and mixture is boiling, about 3 minutes. Remove from heat.

Place mango in a blender, pour in sugar mixture, and blend on medium-high until very smooth, about 1 minute. Pour through a fine mesh strainer set over a medium bowl and, using a rubber spatula, work the mixture through the strainer, discarding any pulp or stringy fibers. Measure 2 cups (475 mL) of the purée (reserve any extra purée for another use); set aside.

Place 1 ¼ cups (300 mL) of the remaining water in a small saucepan over high heat and bring to a boil.

Meanwhile, place the remaining ¾ cup (150 g) sugar, gelatin, and salt in a large mixing bowl, add remaining ½ cup (120 mL) water, and whisk to incorporate, about 30 seconds. Add boiling water and whisk until gelatin and sugar are dissolved, about 1 minute.

Add the 2 cups (475 mL) of mango purée, cream, and lime juice and whisk until evenly combined. Divide the mixture evenly among the ramekins and refrigerate until set, at least 2 hours.

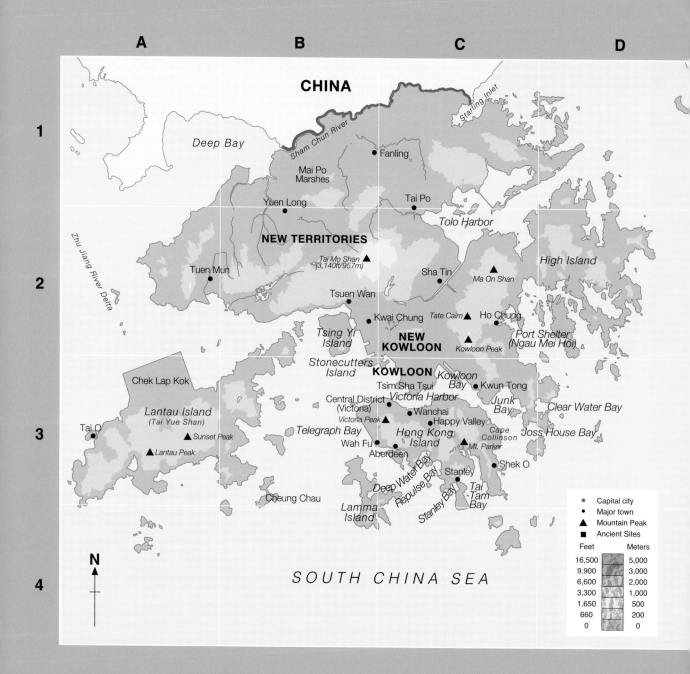

A   **B**   **C**   **D**

1

CHINA

Deep Bay

Sham Chun River

Starling Inlet

• Fanling

Mai Po
Marshes

Yuen Long •

Tai Po •

Tolo Harbor

NEW TERRITORIES

Tai Mo Shan
(3,140ft/957m) ▲

Sha Tin •

▲
Ma On Shan

High Island

Zhu Jiang River Delta

2

Tuen Mun •

Tsuen Wan •

Kwai Chung •

Tate Cairn ▲ Ho Chung
•

Port Shelter
(Ngau Mei Hoi)

Tsing Yi
Island

NEW
KOWLOON

▲
Kowloon Peak

Stonecutters
Island

KOWLOON

Kowloon
Bay

• Kwun Tong

Chek Lap Kok

Tsim Sha Tsui •

Victoria Harbor

Junk
Bay

Clear Water Bay

Central District
(Victoria)

• Wanchai

Tai O •

3

Lantau Island
(Tai Yue Shan)

▲ *Sunset Peak*

▲ *Lantau Peak*

Telegraph Bay

Victoria Peak ▲

Hong Kong
Island

• Happy Valley

Cape
Collinson

Joss House Bay

Wah Fu •

Aberdeen •

▲
Mt. Parker

• Shek O

Deep Water Bay

Stanley •

Cheung Chau

Repulse Bay

Stanley Bay

Tai
Tam
Bay

Lamma
Island

4

N

SOUTH CHINA SEA

	Capital city
	Major town
▲	Mountain Peak
■	Ancient Sites

Feet		Meters
16,500		5,000
9,900		3,000
6,600		2,000
3,300		1,000
1,650		500
660		200
0		0

MAP OF HONG KONG

Aberdeen, C3

Cape
  Collinson, C3
Central
  District, C3
Chek Lap Kok, A3
Cheung Chau, B3
China, A1, B1, C1
Clear
  Water Bay, D3

Deep Bay, A1, B1

Fanling, B1

Happy Valley, C3
High
  Island, D1—D2
Ho Chung, C2
Hong Kong
  Island, B3, C3

Joss House
  Bay, C3, D3
Junk Bay, C3

Kowloon, C3
Kowloon Bay, C3
Kowloon Peak, C2
Kwai Chung, B2
Kwun Tong, C3

Lamma
  Island, B3—B4
Lantau
  Island, A3—B3
Lantau
  Peak, A3, B3

Ma On Shan, C2
Mai Po
  Marshes, B1
Mount Parker, C3

New Kowloon,
  B2—B3, C2—C3
New
  Territories, B2

Port
  Shelter, C2—D2

Repulse Bay, C3

Sha Tin, C2
Sham Chun
  River, B1, C1
Shek O, C3
South China Sea,
  A4, B4, C4, D4
Stanley, C3
Stanley Bay, C3
Starling inlet, C1
Stonecutters
  Island, B3

Sunset Peak, A3

Tai Mo Shan, B2
Tai O, A3
Tai Po, C1—C2
Tai Tam Bay, C3
Tate Cairn, C2
Telegraph Bay, B3
Tolo Harbor, C2
Tsim Sha Tsui, C3
Tsing Yi Island, B2
Tsuen Wan, B2
Tuen Mun, A2

Victoria, B3—C3
Victoria
  Harbor, C3
Victoria Peak, C3

Wah Fu, B3—C3
Wanchai, C3

Yuen
  Long, B1—B2

Zhu Jiang
  River Delta, A2

ECONOMIC HONG KONG

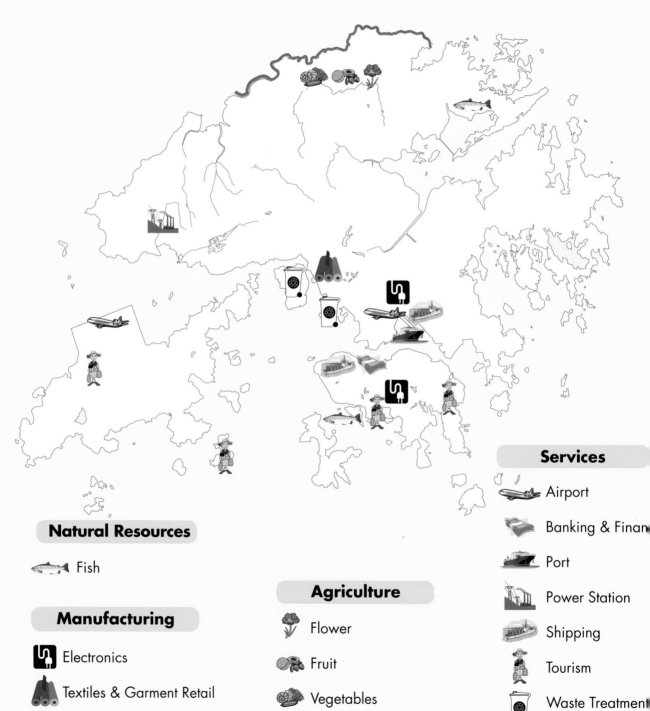

Natural Resources

🐟 Fish

Manufacturing

🔌 Electronics

🧵 Textiles & Garment Retail

Agriculture

🌸 Flower

🍊 Fruit

🥬 Vegetables

Services

✈️ Airport

💵 Banking & Finan

🚢 Port

🏭 Power Station

🚢 Shipping

🧍 Tourism

🗑️ Waste Treatment

ABOUT THE ECONOMY

GROSS DOMESTIC PRODUCT (GDP)
(official exchange rate)
$316.1 billion (2016)

GDP GROWTH
1.4 percent (2016)

GDP BY SECTOR
Agriculture, 0.1 percent
Industry, 7.2 percent
Services, 92.8 percent (2016)

INFLATION RATE
2.6 percent (2016)

LAND USE
Agricultural land, 5 percent;
forest, 0 percent

CURRENCY
HKD (Hong Kong dollar), 1 HKD = 100 cents
Coins: 10, 20, 50 cents
Notes: 10, 20, 50, 100, 500, 1,000 dollars
1 USD = 7.81 HKD (2017)

NATURAL RESOURCES
outstanding deepwater harbor, feldspar

AGRICULTURAL PRODUCTS
Fresh fruits and vegetables, poultry, pork, and fish

INDUSTRY
Banking and financial services, electronics, tourism, shipping, textiles and clothing, plastics

MAJOR EXPORTS
Electrical machinery and appliances, textiles, apparel, footwear, watches and clocks, toys, plastics, precious stones, printed material

MAJOR IMPORTS
Raw materials and semi-manufactures, consumer goods, capital goods, foodstuffs, fuel (most is reexported)

MAIN TRADE PARTNERS
China, Japan, United States, Taiwan, Singapore, South Korea (2015)

WORKFORCE
3.91 million (2016)
Manufacturing, 3.8 percent
Construction, 2.8 percent
Wholesale and retail trade, restaurants, and hotels, 53.3 percent
Financing, insurance, and real estate, 12.5 percent
Transport and communications, 10.1 percent
Community and social services, 17.1 percent

UNEMPLOYMENT RATE
3.6 percent (2016)

POPULATION BELOW POVERTY LINE
19.6 percent (2012)

CULTURAL HONG KONG

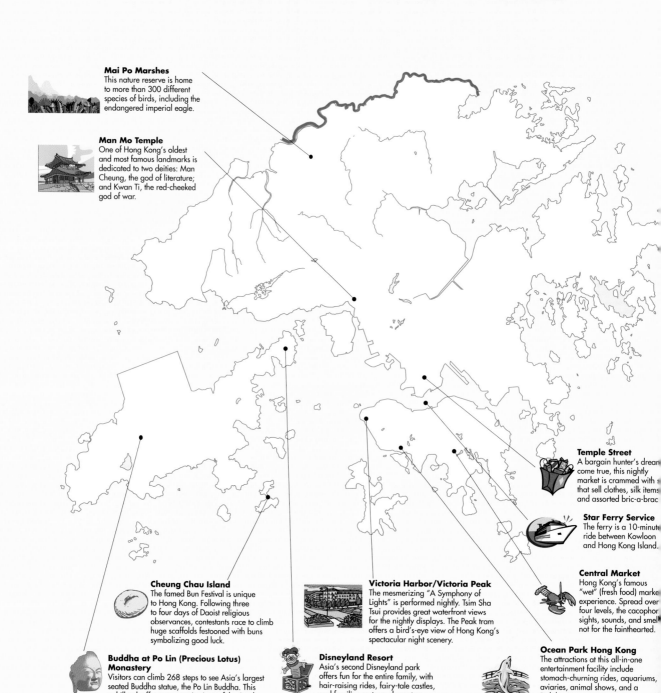

Mai Po Marshes
This nature reserve is home to more than 300 different species of birds, including the endangered imperial eagle.

Man Mo Temple
One of Hong Kong's oldest and most famous landmarks is dedicated to two deities: Man Cheung, the god of literature; and Kwan Ti, the red-cheeked god of war.

Temple Street
A bargain hunter's dream come true, this nightly market is crammed with that sell clothes, silk items and assorted bric-a-brac

Star Ferry Service
The ferry is a 10-minute ride between Kowloon and Hong Kong Island.

Central Market
Hong Kong's famous "wet" (fresh food) marke experience. Spread over four levels, the cacophor sights, sounds, and smel not for the fainthearted.

Cheung Chau Island
The famed Bun Festival is unique to Hong Kong. Following three to four days of Daoist religious observances, contestants race to climb huge scaffolds festooned with buns symbolizing good luck.

Victoria Harbor/Victoria Peak
The mesmerizing "A Symphony of Lights" is performed nightly. Tsim Sha Tsui provides great waterfront views for the nightly displays. The Peak tram offers a bird's-eye view of Hong Kong's spectacular night scenery.

Buddha at Po Lin (Precious Lotus) Monastery
Visitors can climb 268 steps to see Asia's largest seated Buddha statue, the Po Lin Buddha. This uphill trek offers panoramic views of the South China Sea and surrounding islands.

Disneyland Resort
Asia's second Disneyland park offers fun for the entire family, with hair-raising rides, fairy-tale castles, and familiar cartoon characters.

Ocean Park Hong Kong
The attractions at this all-in-one entertainment facility include stomach-churning rides, aquariums, aviaries, animal shows, and a Dolphin University.

ABOUT THE CULTURE

OFFICIAL NAME
Hong Kong Special Administrative Region (SAR) of China

FLAG DESCRIPTION
Red with a white five-petal bauhinia flower in the center

INDEPENDENCE
None (Handed over to China on July 1, 1997)

MAJOR URBAN AREAS
Central, Kowloon, Wan Chai

POPULATION
7.17 million (2016)

URBANIZATION
100 percent

INFANT MORTALITY RATE
2.7 deaths per 1,000 live births (2016)

LIFE EXPECTANCY AT BIRTH
82.9 years (2016)

POPULATION GROWTH RATE
0.35 percent (2016)

ETHNIC GROUPS
Chinese, 93.1 percent; Indonesian, 1.9 percent; Filipino, 1.9 percent; others, 3 percent (2011)

RELIGIONS
Buddhist, Daoist, and local religions, 90 percent; Christian, 10 percent

LANGUAGES
Cantonese (official), 89.5 percent; English (official), 3.5 percent; Mandarin (official), 1.4 percent; other Chinese dialects, 4 percent; others 1.6 percent (2011)

TIMELINE

IN HONG KONG	IN THE WORLD

4000 BCE
Early settlers inhabit the area around Hong Kong.

200 BCE
Unification of Chinese empire; Hong Kong Island is ruled by a governor based in China's Canton province.

CE 1685
British and French merchants start trading tea and silk with Hong Kong.

1000 CE
The Chinese perfect gunpowder and begin to use it in warfare.

1100
Rise of the Incan civilization in Peru

1206–1368
Genghis Khan unifies the Mongols and starts conquest of the world. At its height, the Mongol Empire under Kublai Khan stretches from China to Persia and parts of Europe and Russia.

1558–1603
Reign of Elizabeth I of England

1789–1799
The French Revolution

1842
China defeated in First Opium War; Hong Kong Island is ceded to the British.

1861
China concedes Kowloon Peninsula to Great Britain.

1869
The Suez Canal is opened.

1898
China signs treaty leasing the New Territories to Britain for 99 years.

1914–1919
World War I

1939–1945
World War II

1941
British forces surrender, leading to Japanese occupation of Hong Kong.

1945
Hong Kong reverts to British colonial rule following Japanese defeat at the end of World War II.

1949
Communist Party gains victory in China; refugees flock to Hong Kong.

IN HONG KONG		IN THE WORLD
1950–1953		
United States imposes sanctions on China during the Korean War; Hong Kong develops its own manufacturing base.		
1967		
Hong Kong rocked by political riots arising from the Chinese Cultural Revolution.		**1969**
1975		Neil Armstrong becomes the first human to walk on the moon.
Indochina War leads to influx of 100,000 Vietnamese refugees to the colony.		
1982		
Then–British Prime Minister Margaret Thatcher visits Beijing to discuss Hong Kong's future.		
1984		**1986**
Sino-British Joint Declaration states that Hong Kong will return to Chinese rule in 1997.		Nuclear power disaster at Chernobyl in Ukraine
1988		
Beijing publishes Basic Law guaranteeing the rights of Hong Kong citizens.		
1989		**1991**
More than one million Hong Kongers protest the Tiananmen Square massacre.		Breakup of the Soviet Union
1997		**2001**
Hong Kong becomes a Special Administrative Region (SAR) of China.		Terrorists crash planes in New York, Washington D.C., and Pennsylvania.
2003		**2003**
Severe acute respiratory syndrome (SARS) epidemic brings Hong Kong to a standstill.		War in Iraq begins.
		2008
		US elects first African American president, Barack Obama.
2014		**2015–2016**
Umbrella Movement protests shut down Hong Kong.		ISIS launches terror attacks in Belgium and France.
2017		**2017**
Carrie Lam becomes first woman chief executive of Hong Kong.		Donald Trump becomes US president. Britain begins Brexit process of leaving the EU.

GLOSSARY

char siu
Sweet barbecued pork.

chi
Spirit, energy.

congee
The English name for Cantonese rice porridge ("juk" in Cantonese).

dao (dow, rhymes with now)
In the Daoist religion, the spiritual path that leads to immortality.

dim sum
Dumplings or other foods eaten in small portions, particularly while drinking tea.

Eurasian
People of mixed European and Asian heritage.

expatriate
A person who lives outside his or her own country.

feng shui (fung shuee)
An ancient system of attaining good health and fortune through a harmonious environment.

gweilo (gwy-loh)
Caucasian person (literally "foreign devil").

laisee (ly-see)
Red packets of lucky money given at Chinese New Year and other special occasions.

laissez-faire
The practice of noninterference in the affairs of others; often used to describe a government with minimal involvement in economic affairs.

joss stick
Incense stick; joss means "luck."

junk
A Chinese sailing ship.

mah-jongg
A Chinese game of tiles played by four people.

mooncakes
Pastries filled with sweet lotus paste.

siu ngor (syoo gnaw)
Barbecued goose.

spirit money
Pretend paper money that is burned as an offering to gods or ancestral ghosts.

tai chi
A Chinese martial art characterized by meditative exercises.

weiqi (way-chee)
A Chinese board game.

yang
Energy that is positive and active.

yin
Energy that is negative and passive.

yum cha
To drink tea.

zham cha (tsum chah)
To serve tea.

FOR FURTHER INFORMATION

BOOKS

Bush, Richard C. *Hong Kong in the Shadow of China: Living With the Leviathan.* Washington, DC: Brookings Institution Press, 2016.

Fitzpatrick, Liam, and Jason Gagliardi and Andrew Stone. *DK Eyewitness Travel. Top 10 Hong Kong.* New York: DK Penguin Random House, 2016.

Lonely Planet, *Hong Kong.* Franklin, Tenn.: Lonely Planet, 2017.

Ng, Jason Y. *Hong Kong State of Mind: 37 Views of a City That Doesn't Blink.* Hong Kong: Blacksmith Books, 2015.

DVDS/FILMS

A Simple Life. Well Go USA, 2012.

Chungking Express. Miramax, 1994.

Enter the Dragon. Warner Brothers. 1973.

Fists of Fury. Golden Harvest, 1972.

In the Mood for Love. Paradis Films, 2001.

WEBSITES

BBC News. Hong Kong territory profile. http://www.bbc.com/news/world-asia-pacific-16517764

CIA World Factbook. Hong Kong. https://www.cia.gov/library/publications/the-world-factbook/geos/hk.html

Discover Hong Kong. http://www.discoverhongkong.com/us/index.jsp

GovHK. https://www.gov.hk/en/

New York Times, The. Hong Kong archive. https://www.nytimes.com/topic/destination/hong-kong

BIBLIOGRAPHY

Barber, Elizabeth. "79 Days That Shook Hong Kong." *Time*, December 14, 2014. http://time.com/3632739/hong-kong-umbrella-revolution-photos

Chan, Samuel. "Almost half of Hong Kong parents 'do not have a second baby due to lack of childcare'." *South China Morning Post*, February 24, 2014. http://www.scmp.com/news/hong-kong/article/1433695/almost-half-hong-kong-parents-do-not-have-second-baby-due-lack

Department of Health, government of Hong Kong. "Health Facts of Hong Kong, 2017 edition." http://www.dh.gov.hk/english/statistics/statistics_hs/files/Health_Statistics_pamphlet_E.pdf

Gayle, Damien. "Cage dogs of Hong Kong: The tragedy of tens of thousands living in 6ft by 2ft rabbit hutches—in a city with more Louis Vuitton shops than Paris." *Daily Mail*, January 11, 2012. http://www.dailymail.co.uk/news/article-2084971/Hong-Kongs-cage-homes-Tens-thousands-living-6ft-2ft-rabbit-hutches.html

Haas, Benjamin. "Where the wind blows: how China's dirty air becomes Hong Kong's problem." *The Guardian*, February 16, 2017. https://www.theguardian.com/cities/2017/feb/16/hong-kong-death-trap-dirty-air-pollution-china

Hampshire, Angharad. "Why Hong Kong is failing its young families." *Post Magazine*, October 31, 2015. http://www.scmp.com/magazines/post-magazine/article/1873679/why-hong-kong-failing-its-young-families

Liu, Juliana. "Cantonese v Mandarin: When Hong Kong languages get political." BBC News, June 29, 2017. http://www.bbc.com/news/world-asia-china-40406429

Robson, David. "Hong Kong has a monumental waste problem." BBC Future, April 27, 2017. http://www.bbc.com/future/story/20170427-hong-kong-has-a-monumental-waste-problem

Wong, Cal. "2 Years Later: A Look Back at Hong Kong's Umbrella Movement." *The Diplomat*, September 29, 2016. http://thediplomat.com/2016/09/2-years-later-a-look-back-at-hong-kongs-umbrella-movement

World Health Organization. "Summary of probable SARS cases with onset of illness from 1 November 2002 to 31 July 2003." http://www.who.int/csr/sars/country/table2004_04_21/en

Yeung, Raymond. "Hong Kong housing minister pushes for subdivided flats to be managed by NGOs under pilot scheme." *South China Morning Post*, July 12, 2017. http://www.scmp.com/news/hong-kong/education-community/article/2102239/hong-kong-housing-minister-pushes-subdivided

INDEX

INDEX